20100811

D0929023

IN
AMERICAN
HISTORY

THE CONFEDERACY AND THE CIVIL WAR IN AMERICAN HISTORY

Ann Graham Gaines

Enslow Publishers, Inc.

40 Industrial Road   PO Box 38
Box 398   Aldershot
Berkeley Heights, NJ 07922   Hants GU12 6BP
USA   UK

http://www.enslow.com

Library of Congress Cataloging-in-Publication Data

Gaines, Ann.
      The Confederacy and the Civil War in American history / Ann Graham
      Gaines.
            p. cm.
      Includes bibliographical references (p.) and index.
      Summary: Examines the Confederacy's role in the Civil War, the
      hostility between northern and southern states, and the aftermath of war.
      ISBN 0-7660-1417-7
            1. Confederate States of America—History Juvenile literature.
      2. United States—History—Civil War, 1861–1865 Juvenile literature.
      3. United States—History—Civil War, 1861–1865—Influence Juvenile
      literature. [1. Confederate States of America—History. 2. United States—
      History—Civil War, 1861–1865.] I. Title.
      E487.G25   2000
      973.7'13—dc21
                                                                    99-16688
                                                                    CIP

Printed in the United States of America

10 9 8 7 6 5 4 3 2

To Our Readers: We have done our best to make sure all Internet addresses in
this book were active and appropriate when we went to press. However, the
author and the publisher have no control over and assume no liability for the
material available on those Internet sites or on other Web sites they may link to.
Any comments or suggestions can be sent by e-mail to comments@enslow.com or
to the address on the back cover.

Illustration Credits: Carol Belanger Grafton, *Authentic Civil War Illustrations*
(New York: Dover Publications, Inc., 1995), pp. 33, 54; Enslow Publishers, Inc.,
pp. 10, 23, 30, 42, 45; *Frank Leslie's Illustrated Newspaper,* April 15, 1863, p. 111;
Harper's Weekly, November 22, 1862, p. 74; *Harper's Weekly*, April 4, 1863, p. 98;
Library of Congress, pp. 6, 17, 21, 38, 61, 73, 91, 105; Mathew Brady et al., *Civil
War Military Leaders* (Mineola, N.Y.: Dover Publications, Inc., 1998), pp. 8, 36,
103; National Archives, pp. 12, 28; Reproduced from the *Dictionary of American
Portraits*, Published by Dover Publications, Inc., in 1967, pp. 37, 79.

Cover Illustration: Mathew Brady et al., *Civil War Military Leaders* (Mineola,
N.Y.: Dover Publications, Inc., 1998).

Every effort has been made to locate the copyright owners of all the pictures in
this book. If due acknowledgment has not been made, we sincerely regret the
omission.

★ CONTENTS ★

On April 12, 1861, telegrams spread alarming news around the world. The next day, in St. Paul, Minnesota, a typical newspaper headline screamed: "THE WAR BEGUN."[1] Deliberately starting what modern Americans call the Civil War, the Confederacy—the new nation formed by seven Southern states just three months earlier—had fired cannons on United States soldiers inside Fort Sumter, located on an island at the mouth of Charleston Harbor.

A NEW NATION AT WAR

When South Carolina became the first state to secede—or withdraw—from the Union in December 1860, the United States Army had still been building Fort Sumter. There were also two other American forts near Charleston. Before secession, residents of South Carolina had not objected to having federal troops stationed in the forts. But when South Carolina declared itself independent from the United States, its citizens expected those troops to leave. After all, in the opinion of Southerners, secession meant that Forts Sumter and Moultrie and Castle Pinckney no longer belonged to the United States.[2] Because they were located on South

ABBEVILLE
BANNER
EXTRA.

Passed unanimously at 1.15 o'clock, P. M. December 20th, 1860.

AN ORDINANCE

To dissolve the Union between the State of South Carolina and other States united with her under the compact entitled " The Constitution of the United States of America."

We, the People of the State of South Carolina, in Convention assembled, do declare and ordain, and it is hereby declared and ordained,

That the Ordinance adopted by us in Convention, on the twenty-third day of May, in the year of our Lord one thousand seven hundred and eighty-eight, whereby the Constitution of the United States of America was ratified, and also, all Acts and parts of Acts of the General Assembly of this State, ratifying amendments of the said Constitution, are hereby repealed; and that the union now subsisting between South Carolina and other States, under the name of " The United States of America," is hereby dissolved.

THE

UNION
IS
DISSOLVED!

Newspapers trumpeted the news of South Carolina's secession from the Union of the states.

Carolina soil, they were part of the new, independent nation.

Major Robert Anderson, the United States Army commander of Fort Moultrie, did not want to give the forts up. He realized, however, that he could not hold Fort Moultrie. A large fort, it could easily be taken from the rear; local militiamen might attack it from nearby sand hills.[3] So late one night, under the cover of darkness, Anderson, along with sixty soldiers, loaded Fort Moultrie's supplies into boats and rowed to Fort Sumter. The single officer at Castle Pinckney joined Anderson at Fort Sumter, too.

For five months, Anderson commanded the combined force of sixty-eight Union soldiers who remained in Fort Sumter. In the meantime, the new Confederate States of America established its own government in February 1861. The continued Union occupation of Fort Sumter became a matter of great symbolic importance to both the North and the South. Towns from all over South Carolina sent members of their local militias to bear arms against Fort Sumter. Eventually, six thousand South Carolinians surrounded the fort. Confederate Army General P.G.T. Beauregard commanded these forces. Ironically, he had been trained in the use of artillery by Anderson, at the United States Military Academy at West Point.

Under Beauregard's direction, soldiers stationed cannons in eleven batteries on the shores closest to the island on which Fort Sumter sat. Batteries formed a semicircle around the Union soldiers.[4] The soldiers at

General P.G.T. Beauregard commanded the Confederate forces during the attack on Fort Sumter.

Fort Sumter could receive no supplies or reinforcements of men. When the Union Navy vessel *Star of the West* attempted to enter Charleston Harbor to bring supplies to Fort Sumter, the Confederates immediately fired at it, forcing it to retreat.

Debate raged in the North about what action President Abraham Lincoln should take regarding the South in general and Fort Sumter in particular. Union General Winfield Scott told Lincoln that, if he wanted the United States to continue to hold the fort, it would take a large fleet of ships and twenty-five thousand troops to resupply the men there. He, along with most members of the Cabinet, agreed that the time had come to abandon Fort Sumter.

Lincoln still had to decide, but William H. Seward, secretary of state, agreed with the Cabinet's thinking. Seward went behind Lincoln's back and sent messages to the Confederates, promising them that the Union would soon abandon the fort. He then tried to persuade Lincoln to let him make and execute plans for the fort's abandonment. Lincoln declined the offer. Though he greatly respected Seward's ability and intellect, he resented his tactics.[5]

The Cabinet may have wanted to abandon Sumter, but public support in the North ran high for Anderson and his garrison. On April 6, Lincoln made up his mind. He had hoped that the Union would be reunited. He continued to pray for peace, but he had decided he would risk war by ordering that supplies be sent to Fort Sumter. He notified the governor of South Carolina of his intent. He added that, as long as the Confederates did not attack the fort or the fleet sent to resupply it, he would not send more soldiers or arms.

Members of the Confederate government disagreed about their response. Secretary of State Robert Toombs did not want Confederate forces to fire on Fort Sumter. Other secessionists, however, wanted to attack. Some Virginians, whose state had not yet seceded, promised that an attack would bring them into the Confederacy. Confederate Secretary of War Leroy P. Walker and President Jefferson Davis settled the matter when they sent General Beauregard, in command of Charleston's Confederate forces, a telegram ordering him to "reduce the fort."[6]

By this time, residents of Charleston had begun to realize that the crisis at Fort Sumter was coming to a head. All over town, people indulged in wild, happy behavior. On April 11, Mary Chesnut, the wife of a

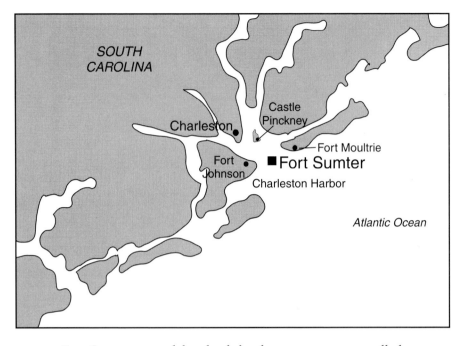

Fort Sumter, owned by the federal government, controlled the entrance to the Charleston, South Carolina, harbor. It was of special symbolic importance to the new Confederacy.

prominent Confederate, along with her family and friends, enjoyed what she called in her diary "the merriest, maddest dinner we have had yet. . . . And so we fool on, into the black cloud ahead of us."[7]

In the middle of the night on April 11–12, 1861, four representatives of the Confederate government climbed into a boat and rowed out to Fort Sumter, where they delivered an official message to Major Anderson. The message gave him until 4 A.M. to surrender. If Anderson failed to do so, Confederate cannons would start to fire upon the fort. Anderson and his officers discussed their situation for three hours and then responded to the ultimatum: They would not surrender.

At 4:30 A.M. on April 12, 1861, the Civil War began when Confederate General Beauregard ordered his men to fire on Fort Sumter. Mary Chesnut, remembering the sudden huge noise of the cannons, recorded in her diary: "April 12 . . . the heavy booming of a cannon. I sprang out of bed, and on my knees prostrate I prayed as I have never prayed before."[8] Over and over, cannons fired on Fort Sumter from three sides. All that day and into the next, residents of Charleston gathered to watch the shelling. Anderson and his men fired back, but they possessed far fewer guns than the Confederate forces.

On April 13, they ran up the white flag of surrender. They had endured thirty-four hours under fire.[9] A total of 3,341 shells had landed around them. Cannonballs had destroyed Fort Sumter's front gate and damaged its walls. Its chimneys and towers had been knocked down, and some of its cannons had been blasted off their mounts. On April 14, Anderson and his men marched out of Fort Sumter. The next day, they were ferried to a United States Navy ship out in the Atlantic that soon sailed north, back to Union territory.[10]

The Union and Confederate public greeted the news of the surrender of Fort Sumter differently. Northerners generally believed that the situation demanded vengeance. As one Boston resident wrote after the attack on Fort Sumter, "it would have been

In April 1861, Confederate forces fired on Fort Sumter, seen here flying the Confederate flag. The attack marked the start of the Civil War.

dangerous for anyone to have said a word in favor of secession, even in the worst parts of the city. . . ."[11] Many Southerners actually looked forward to the war that they considered now under way. After hearing reactions on the part of his friends and neighbors, the editor of the *Montgomery Advertiser* wrote,

> The intelligence [news] that Fort Sumter has surrendered to the Confederate forces . . . sent a thrill of joy to the heart of every true friend of the South. The face of every southern man was brighter, his step lighter, and his bearing prouder than it had ever been before.[12]

On both sides of the Mason-Dixon line—the boundary dividing free states from slave states—men lined up to enlist in the Union and Confederate armies. Women began sewing flags and uniforms; generals and politicians held meetings to plan their strategies. The Union hoped to bring down the Confederacy within a matter of months. Many Confederates also believed that the war would be short. But they believed they would win, and their new nation would endure for centuries. They saw themselves as reformers. The United States had lost its way, they said. The Founding Fathers had recognized slavery and guaranteed states' rights in the Constitution.[13] The Confederates believed they were beginning again, acting on the Founders' principles. They were sure their cause was just and their success was guaranteed.

2

BEGINNINGS OF THE CONFEDERACY

Officially known as the Confederate States of America, the Confederacy was founded in 1861. However, the string of events that led to its establishment started much earlier. In 1860, white Americans in general were blessed with a sense of well-being. They felt happy and prosperous and they believed that their children's lives would be even better than their own. But, according to historian Bruce Catton, an explosion was about to occur: "[Infinite] change was beginning, and problems left unsolved too long would presently make the change explosive, so that the old landscape would be blown to bits forever, with a bewildered people left to salvage what they could."[1]

On the eve of the Civil War, most people lived on farms or in small towns. The nation's economy was still based on the products of farms rather than factories. This would be the last time in American history, however, that this would be true. The North had been developing a very different sort of society since the early 1800s. Although agriculture was still important in the North, industry was growing and cities were expanding. Immigrants were pouring in, hoping to find new opportunity in America.

From the outside, life in the South appeared very different. To this day, many Americans carry in their minds a vision of what they call the Old South, though this vision never actually existed. This picture is one of moonlight and magnolias, of huge mansions, with stately white columns, surrounded by hundred-year-old oak trees—of Tara, Scarlett O'Hara's plantation in *Gone With the Wind*. The white people in this image are always at leisure. Slaves do all the household chores. Dashing gentlemen ride out into the fields, but slaves work the acres of growing cotton or tobacco. Some planters did live like this, and writers and politicians promoted theirs as the genuine South. But for the majority of the Southern population, this image was simply not true: They did not own slaves. They could not afford to buy or keep them.

Slavery

Slavery had existed all over colonial America for centuries, but few Northerners owned slaves by the early nineteenth century. Slavery had become an issue during the American Revolution. After it ended, many slave owners from both the North and the South freed their slaves.

Northern state legislatures then began to pass gradual emancipation laws. A 1799 New York law, for example, provided that, from that point on, all slaves born in the state must be freed by age twenty-five for males and age twenty-one for females.[2] By 1810, three fourths of the black population of the North was free. Twenty years later, almost nobody in the North remained in slavery.[3] Emancipation was considered acceptable in that region partly because the North's many merchants and small farmers did not see a need for slave labor to make a profit or to survive. There were plenty of immigrants willing to take low-paying factory jobs in the city and the majority of Northern farmers grew mainly to feed their families, not to export huge cash crops.

In the South, on the other hand, plantation owners considered slaves absolutely essential. With the invention of the cotton gin (which quickly and easily removed seeds from and cleaned the cotton that earlier had taken much longer to process) by Eli Whitney in 1793, the short-staple cotton the South grew came into huge demand. Much Southern soil was poor. Constant hard work in harsh conditions was needed to grow crops like cotton, tobacco, rice, and sugarcane. Slavery had to continue if planters were to continue to profit by providing the world with the cotton and other commodities it demanded. In 1860, the United States exported cotton worth $191 million, making up close to 60 percent of all American exports.[4]

The decline in Northern slavery was accompanied by the rise of an abolition movement. Abolitionists hoped to get rid of slavery, and their movement arose in the North in the 1830s. Although, at first, the movement was considered too radical for most

A big demand for cotton came about after the invention of the cotton gin. Southerners depended on slavery to support them in exporting cotton, a business that amounted to $191 million in 1860. Here, black slaves work at separating cotton on a Southern plantation.

Northerners, it gradually won support over the years. William Lloyd Garrison was one of the leaders of the crusade for the abolition of slavery. He labeled all slave owners sinners in the eyes of God. In 1831, he started publishing *The Liberator*, an abolitionist newspaper. In 1833, he helped found the American Anti-Slavery Society, whose membership rose to almost 250,000 within five years. Its members wrote and spoke about the dangers of slavery. They also helped slaves escape to the safety of the Northern states and Canada on the Underground Railroad, a network of people who helped escaped slaves heading north to freedom by hiding them and providing them places to rest and food to eat.

The abolition movement was unpopular, and even violently attacked, at first, but the movement did grow. Most Southerners, however, failed to join the cause. Many abolitionists failed to acknowledge that the end of slavery would mean the collapse of the Southern economy. In the face of the very vocal abolitionists, Southerners became ever more committed to maintaining what they called their "peculiar institution." They even went so far as to argue that slaves were actually not oppressed, but fortunate to be held in slavery! Thornton Stringfellow, a Baptist minister in the South, was among those who claimed that slave owners were generally loving people who offered their slaves care and protection. Slaves lived under better conditions than workers in Great Britain and the Northern cities, Stringfellow wrote: "Their condition . . . is now better than that of any equal number of laborers on earth and is daily improving."[5] Southerners also argued that slaves benefited from being introduced to Christianity by their masters.

The Division Grows Wider

In the mid-nineteenth century, certain groups in the North and South disagreed about the role the federal government should play in the lives of American citizens. Most Northerners wanted aid from the government—manufacturers wanted tariffs to help keep cheap European imports out of the American marketplace, for example. (Tariffs are duties, or extra money, governments charge on certain goods being imported or exported.) Northerners also wanted the federal government to provide money to build the railroads required to create an industrial economy. Southerners, in contrast, wanted the federal government to do as little as possible for them—or to them. They believed the individual states had the right to handle most matters. Southerners fought against tariffs, since they wanted to buy cheap European imports rather than the more expensive products of the North. Southerners became afraid that, as the North's population grew (due to immigration from Europe), that part of the country would soon control the federal government and force changes upon the South.[6]

The trouble over tariffs led the North and the South to argue over states' rights. According to Southerners, the Founding Fathers had intended the United States to be a union of sovereign (self-governing) states. In 1787, delegates to the Constitutional Convention in Philadelphia adopted the Constitution of the United States. At that time, members of the Federalist party were very powerful. They did not want the United States to function as a collection of independent states. Instead, they wanted national and state governments to share authority. They also thought the national government should have the final say in cases of disagreement between the states and the federal government. By 1800, members of a new political party, the Democratic-Republicans, were protesting that the Federalists wanted to give the national government too much power.

Over the years, arguments over the issue of state versus national power became more and more severe. At times, disagreements between the two sides threatened to tear apart the nation. Congressman John C. Calhoun became famous for his defense of states' rights in the 1820s. In 1828, he wrote a pamphlet arguing against a new tariff that had hurt the South. He based his argument on the idea of nullification, a theory that said states could refuse to follow laws they believed were unconstitutional. Calhoun claimed that, because the tariff was unconstitutional, states had the right to ignore the federal law that instituted it. His pamphlet created an enormous stir. President Andrew Jackson, who believed the national government was supreme to the states, toasted the nation, saying, "Our Federal Union! It *must* and *shall be* preserved!"[7]

John Calhoun, congressman and champion of states' rights, urged Southern unity.

Going against Jackson's wishes, the state of South Carolina tried to nullify tariffs that the federal government had imposed in 1828 and 1832. It also decided that the state would not collect customs duties for the federal government.[8] Kentucky Senator Henry Clay eased this sectional crisis with the Compromise of 1833, which lowered the tariffs South Carolinians hated. In turn, they gave up nullification. Americans credited the Compromise of 1833 with saving the nation, and Clay was called the "Great Compromiser."[9] Calhoun, on the other hand, began to try to bring Southern politicians into a single camp. He would continue to campaign for Southern unity until his death in 1850.

The states' rights issue was a serious one in affairs between the North and the South. But historians generally conclude that politicians might have settled the nation's differences if it had not been for slavery.

Historian Bruce Catton wrote, "Slavery poisoned the whole situation."[10]

Slavery in the West

Early in the history of the United States, the question of whether slavery should be permitted to expand into new western territories became a political issue. The question first arose in regard to the vast lands west of the Mississippi River that the United States acquired as part of the Louisiana Purchase in 1803. In 1820, the Missouri Compromise allowed Missouri to enter the Union as a slave state, but decreed that slavery would be prohibited in territory north of Missouri's southern boundary, at latitude 36°30'. After the United States defeated Mexico in the Mexican War and signed the Treaty of Guadalupe-Hidalgo in 1848, it again acquired vast new territories—including what became the present-day states of California, Arizona, and New Mexico. Americans everywhere argued furiously over a bill, introduced by Congressman David Wilmot in August 1846, that would have prohibited slavery in any of these lands.

The Wilmot Proviso failed to pass. To solve the problem, longtime politician Henry Clay and others came up with the Compromise of 1850. Under it, California entered the Union as a free state. The New Mexico Territory (which included present-day Arizona) was also created, with the requirement that a vote of settlers there (popular sovereignty) would later decide whether slavery would be legal. The Compromise of 1850 also outlawed slave trading in Washington, D.C., the nation's capital. As part of the compromise, the tough new Fugitive Slave Law was also passed, benefiting slave owners by making it legal for professional slave hunters to go north and capture escaped slaves.

Despite the hopes of both North and South, the Compromise of 1850 failed to settle the issue of slavery. Abolitionists vigorously protested the Fugitive Slave Law, whereas Southerners continued to hope they could expand their peculiar institution into new American territories.

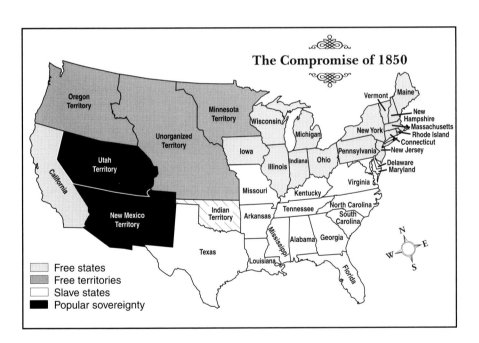

The Compromise of 1850 admitted California to the Union as a free state, opened new western territories to popular sovereignty, and put the new Fugitive Slave Law into effect. It was one of many measures passed over the years to try to ease tensions between the North and the South.

In 1854, Congress debated the Kansas-Nebraska Bill, proposed by Senator Stephen A. Douglas because he wanted a transcontinental railroad built across the United States. The bill would create the new territories of Kansas and Nebraska, which would be public lands over which a railroad could be built if a northern route were chosen. Southerners wanted the transcontinental railroad to cross Texas and New Mexico instead of Kansas and Nebraska. Nevertheless, Southern congressmen voted for Douglas's act because it included a provision stating that popular sovereignty—the vote of local settlers—would decide whether these territories entered the Union as slave states or free states. By allowing for the possibility of slave states above the 36°30' line, the bill would also remove the Missouri Compromise's ban on slavery in the bulk of the Louisiana Territory.

Red-Hot Debate

The effect of the Kansas-Nebraska Act, passed in 1854, was to remove moderation from the debate over slavery. Now extremists became more vocal on both sides. By this time, the existing political parties had begun to fall apart because of disagreement over slavery. The new Republican party came into power as a response to the Kansas-Nebraska Act and the growing controversy over the expansion of slavery. It received great support from voters who did not support slavery. Eventually, it came to include former Northern Whigs, Northern Democrats, and Know-Nothings—all those

BE IT ENACTED . . . THE TERRITORY OF NEBRASKA . . . WHEN ADMITTED AS A STATE OR STATES, THE SAID TERRITORY, OR ANY PORTION OF THE SAME, SHALL BE RECEIVED INTO THE UNION WITH OR WITHOUT SLAVERY, AS THEIR CONSTITUTION MAY PRESCRIBE AT THE TIME OF THEIR ADMISSION: . . .

AND BE IT FURTHER ENACTED, . . . THAT NOTHING CONTAINED HEREIN SHALL BE CONSTRUED TO REVIVE OR PUT IN FORCE ANY LAW OF REGULATION WHICH MAY HAVE EXISTED PRIOR TO THE ACT OF MARCH 6, 1820, EITHER PROTECTING, ESTABLISHING, PROHIBITING, OR ABOLISHING SLAVERY. . . .

AND BE IT FURTHER ENACTED, . . . THE TERRITORY OF KANSAS . . . WHEN ADMITTED AS A STATE OR STATES, THE SAID TERRITORY, OR ANY PORTION OF THE SAME, SHALL BE RECEIVED INTO THE UNION WITH OR WITHOUT SLAVERY, AS THEIR CONSTITUTION MAY PRESCRIBE AT THE TIME OF THEIR ADMISSION: . . .[11]

The Kansas-Nebraska Act of 1854 further divided the nation over the issue of slavery's expanding into the western territories.

people from the older parties now united to express their disapproval of slavery's expansion. The growth of the Republican party meant a sectional—all-Northern—political alliance had formed. The Republicans were not, for the most part, abolitionists. They did include a large number of Free-Soilers, who opposed the extension of slavery into new territories, regardless of whether they liked slavery itself.

In the mid-1850s, the Kansas Territory became known as Bleeding Kansas. Proslavery and antislavery factions fought violently to try to make the territory either a slave state or free. Eventually, two rival governments, each apparently backed by popular vote, came into existence. Popular sovereignty had failed to decide the issue of whether or not slavery should be legal there. As a result of the outbreak of violence in Kansas, the Republican party became dedicated to the idea of free soil, and its popularity increased all over the North.

In 1857, the United States Supreme Court added to the debate with its *Dred Scott* decision. It ruled that a slave who had lived for several years with his master in free states and territories was not free. The Court stated that a black person could not become a citizen of the United States and thus had no right to sue (Scott had sued for his freedom). The Court ruled that the Constitution protected slavery, which could not be prohibited in any territory. Therefore, the Court ruled, the Missouri Compromise had been unconstitutional.

Debate in the political arena then became even more heated. Abraham Lincoln entered the picture when he ran for the United States Senate against Stephen A. Douglas, author of the Kansas-Nebraska Act. The two engaged in a famous series of debates. Lincoln forced Douglas to state publicly that he believed slavery could exist in a territory only if its legislature enacted laws protecting slavery. Unless such laws were passed, slavery could not exist. Thus Douglas came out against the decision of the Supreme Court. He won the election, but the South was outraged. The Democratic party came close to splitting in two over the slavery issue.

In 1859, John Brown, a radical white abolitionist, tried to start a slave insurrection. His plan was to seize weapons from the federal arsenal at Harpers Ferry, Virginia (now in West Virginia), and pass them on to slaves, who would then revolt against their masters. He was captured, tried for treason, and hanged. His actions inspired thousands of Northerners to join the crusade to free the South's slaves, but they also terrified white Southerners, whose worst fear was a mass slave insurrection.

The Election of Abraham Lincoln

Now differences between the North and the South became impossible to overcome. In 1860, Republican Abraham Lincoln was elected president of the United States. His was hardly an overwhelming victory, however. The Democratic party had finally split in 1860.

Militant abolitionist John Brown enraged the South with his attack on the arsenal at Harpers Ferry, Virginia. Although he was hanged for treason, his attempted slave rebellion pushed the South closer to starting a civil war.

In a meeting at Charleston, South Carolina, delegates from seven states had formed a Southern Democratic faction. Southern Democrats supported presidential candidate John C. Breckinridge. Northern Democrats supported Stephen Douglas. Complicating the situation even further, John Bell ran as a member of the Constitutional Union party, a new party that took no stand on the issue of the extension of slavery. Instead, it simply called for the preservation of the Union. Lincoln did win more votes than any of his opponents. He did not, however, win a majority of the popular vote. He won the election in the electoral college, where delegates from the states vote for the president, without any support from the South.[12] His name had not even appeared on the ballot in Southern states.

Immediately after the election, the secession movement, which had been slowly growing throughout the South, became stronger. Senator John J. Crittenden tried to head off the crisis by proposing what was called the Crittenden Compromise. Under it, a constitutional amendment would have put the Missouri Compromise line back in effect. Slavery would have been allowed in all future states south of 36°30' latitude, and the Fugitive Slave Law would have been strengthened. Although the Crittenden Compromise eventually inspired a convention to propose seven amendments to the Constitution, it never actually amounted to anything. The Senate voted against the constitutional amendments, and the House of Representatives would not even consider them.

Beginning of Secession

On December 20, 1860, South Carolina became the first Southern state to secede from the United States with a unanimous vote by delegates at a convention. For only a short time, it stood alone as the Palmetto Republic. More states soon followed. A total of seven states—South Carolina, Mississippi, Florida, Alabama, Georgia, Louisiana, and Texas—voted to secede in the forty-three days between December 20, 1860, and February 1, 1861. In each case, the state legislature called a special convention, where delegates voted on the measure. In Texas, voters approved the decision of its secession convention.

When Abraham Lincoln was elected, the Union included thirty-three states. By the time he was

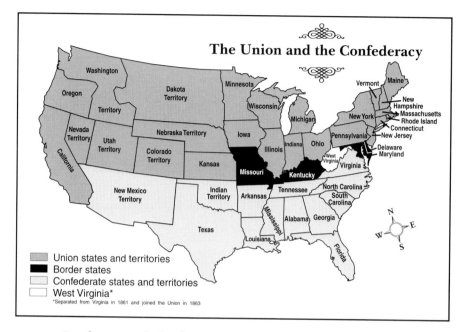

The Union and the Confederacy

Union states and territories
Border states
Confederate states and territories
West Virginia*
*Separated from Virginia in 1861 and joined the Union in 1863

By the time of Abraham Lincoln's inauguration in March 1861, seven states had seceded from the Union and joined the Confederacy. Others would eventually follow.

inaugurated, that number had fallen to twenty-six, according to Southerners. Lincoln, however, still considered himself the president of all thirty-three states. He denied that any state had the right to secede.

In the months ahead, the states that had seceded would form a new nation and embark upon a mission. The new Confederacy sought to establish a better government, in keeping with what Southerners believed to have been the ideals of the Founding Fathers of the United States.

A NEW NATION IS BORN

When they seceded from the United States, the states of South Carolina, Alabama, Mississippi, Florida, Georgia, Louisiana, and Texas briefly became independent republics. However, the Southern states had begun to discuss the formation of a new nation even before secession began. In October 1860, when it looked likely that Abraham Lincoln would win the presidential election, South Carolina's governor, William Henry Gist, wrote to the governors of neighboring states, proposing that they all secede together. His proposal failed. Nevertheless, talk of cooperation among the Southern states continued.

On December 31, 1860, the delegates at the South Carolina secession convention (which had already voted to secede) passed a series of resolutions providing for a convention to be held in Montgomery, Alabama, in February 1861. All seceded states would be invited to send delegates.[1] The purpose of the convention would be to establish a confederacy—a union—and to draw up a new constitution. The South Carolinians believed it absolutely essential that the new government be in place by the time Abraham Lincoln was inaugurated. Montgomery—the capital of Alabama and still a very small city at that time—had been selected as the meeting place because of its central location.

The Montgomery Convention

Response to South Carolina's invitation was favorable. South Carolina's proposal appeared to other states as a "complete plan of confederation, capable of being speedily put into operation."[2] Secessionists also supported the plan because they hoped that, once a new Southern nation was in place, other states would be persuaded to secede.

Forty-three delegates, from six of the seven states that had already seceded, arrived for the Montgomery convention. On February 4, 1861, the convention voted in favor of establishing the Confederate States of America. Seven delegates from Texas, the seventh state to secede, arrived after the convention had already begun.[3]

Once the delegates voted to create the nation, they became the members of its Provisional, or temporary, Congress, which remained in its first session through March 16.[4] The new congressmen would then return to their home states for a vacation. A second session was scheduled to open in May 1861.

The Constitution

On February 5, 1861, the Provisional Congress appointed Christopher G. Memminger, a delegate

The State House in Montgomery, Alabama, was used as the first capital of the seceding states because of its central location.

from South Carolina, as head of a committee in charge of writing a constitution for the new nation. In fact, Memminger had brought a draft of a proposed constitution with him to the convention.[5] Two days later, the committee members submitted a report to the new Congress. The Provisional Constitution of the Confederate States of America was approved on February 8.[6] The permanent constitution was approved by Congress on March 12. It was then ratified, or approved, by the member states.[7]

The new Confederate Constitution called for the government to include executive, legislative, and judicial branches, just as in the United States. The major differences between the new nation and the United States, as spelled out in the Confederate Constitution, were the Confederacy's guarantee of the right to own slaves; its provision for a single six-year presidential term; and its granting of seats in Congress to Cabinet members, should they wish one.[8] The new constitution also declared each of the Confederate states sovereign and independent, meaning that they could secede again if they disagreed with the policies of the new government. It provided slave owners the right to take slaves anywhere within the Confederacy, and it also included a fugitive slave clause. It prohibited the exclusion of free states, should any wish to join the Confederacy. Finally, it allowed for fairly easy amendment of the Constitution: The Confederate Congress would have to summon a constitutional convention if the states called for it to do so. Two thirds of the nation's states—as opposed to the three quarters called for in the United States Constitution—were required to ratify amendments in order for them to become law.

The Presidency

Even as it approved a constitution, the Congress worked on choosing a provisional president. The delegates decided not to hold a general election right away, so the matter was not put to a vote among the Confederate population. At first, there were several names considered for the post. They included Howell Cobb of Georgia, who served as the Provisional Congress's presiding officer. Robert Toombs, another

Georgian, was a possibility, but he lost support after he appeared drunk in public two days before the final vote for president was cast.[9]

On February 9, 1861, the delegates elected Jefferson Davis, born in Kentucky but a longtime resident of Mississippi, as provisional president of the Confederate States of America. Davis had already had a distinguished political career in the United States. After a career in the army, he had been elected to the House of Representatives in 1845. He resigned from Congress to fight in the Mexican War, in which he became a hero. Upon his return in 1847, he was chosen to fill a vacant seat in the United States Senate. In 1853, he joined President Franklin Pierce's Cabinet as secretary of war. In 1857, he was reelected to the Senate, where he championed Southern rights. On January 19, 1861, along with other congressmen and senators, he left his seat in the Senate for good. Davis made an especially memorable speech that day, filled with sorrow over the parting: "Whatever of offense there has been to me, I leave here. I carry with me no hostile remembrance. Whatever offense I have given, . . . I have, Senators, in this hour of our parting, to offer you my apology."[10] He expressed his hope that his former colleagues would allow the Southern states to leave the Union in peace. But he acknowledged the likelihood of war and declared that, should it come, "[Southerners] will invoke the God of our fathers, who delivered them from the power of the lion, to protect us from the ravages of the bear. . . ."[11]

As a United States senator and as the president of the Confederate States of America, Jefferson Davis championed states' rights.

Less than a week after the establishment of the Confederate States, on February 10, Jefferson Davis received a telegram notifying him that he had been elected provisional president. His wife, Varina, remembered that, when he read it, "he looked so grieved that I feared some evil had befallen our family. After a few minutes, he told me [what it contained], as a man might speak of a sentence of death."[12] Nevertheless, Davis accepted the position.

The Montgomery convention elected Alexander Stephens as vice president. A tiny, sickly man—never weighing more than one hundred pounds—he sat stoop-shouldered. His face was already wrinkled, although he would turn only forty-nine the day he was sworn into office. A lawyer by profession, Stephens had a brilliant mind. He had already proven himself an effective leader when he served in the House of Representatives for close to twenty years. Stephens had gained

Alexander H. Stephens was elected vice president of the Confederate States.

According to his wife, Varina (right), when Jefferson Davis told her that he had been elected provisional president of the Confederate States, he spoke as if it were a death sentence.

notoriety in the North when, in a speech he delivered in Savannah, Georgia, before the war began, he said of the Confederacy: "its foundations are laid, its corner-stone rests, upon the great truth that the Negro is not equal to the white man; subordination to the superior race is his natural and moral condition."[13]

The Inauguration

Because Stephens was already at the Montgomery convention, having been a delegate, he was inaugurated on February 11.[14] Davis arrived on February 16 and was inaugurated two days later. It was a joyous day in many ways. War between the Confederacy and the United States seemed possible, but had not yet begun. Ten thousand excited people watched the inauguration parade, listening to a band play "Dixie."[15] Davis took his oath of office and gave a stirring speech in which he appealed to the North to leave the South alone. On March 4, Abraham Lincoln would be inaugurated as Davis's Northern counterpart, the president of the United States. In April, Confederate soldiers would fire upon Fort Sumter, and both Davis and Lincoln would be presidents of nations at war.

The Cabinet

After the inauguration, Davis began to select the men who would be the advisors in his Cabinet. His was a difficult task, in part because so many politicians hoped to get positions and also because Davis believed his Cabinet needed to represent the Confederacy's geography. Initially, he chose one man from each Confederate state to be part of his Cabinet.

Davis appointed Christopher G. Memminger of South Carolina, who had headed the committee that wrote the Confederate Constitution, as secretary of the treasury. A lawyer, Memminger was a brilliant man who worked very hard. But his job, controlling the government's finances, proved impossible. Although Memminger tried to keep the Confederate government's budget balanced, the nation soon ran out of money. He had to authorize the printing of a huge amount of paper money that was not backed by specie (gold or silver). This caused inflation to skyrocket. Nevertheless, he stayed in office for more than three years.[16]

Robert Toombs of Georgia served as the first secretary of state, overseeing the Confederacy's relations with foreign countries. Within a month of taking office, he sent commissioners to England, France, and other nations in Europe, to try to negotiate alliances for the new nation. He would find his job extremely frustrating, however, and would resign after less than six months to take an army position.[17]

As secretary of war, Davis chose Leroy Pope Walker of Alabama, who had to turn his attention immediately to assembling an army to face the threat of war. Davis, who himself had a lot of war experience, planned to assist Walker. Walker's task was also eased somewhat by the fact that each of the Confederate states already had militias—private armies made up of volunteers—that could be expected to supply regiments.

Nevertheless, Walker's was a daunting task, as he tried to find supplies and arm the troops. The army suffered an immediate shortage of both arms and ammunition. Like Toombs, Walker also soon resigned. A hundred years later, historian Bell Irvin Wiley characterized him as "sickly and inept."[18]

Stephen R. Mallory of Florida, on the other hand, did an able job as secretary of the Navy. He set out at once to build the fleet the Confederacy lacked.

Finally, Davis appointed Judah P. Benjamin of Louisiana as attorney general and John H. Reagan of Texas as postmaster general. By the end of the Civil War, Reagan would be the only man to have remained in his Cabinet position throughout the entire war.[19] Despite the fact that, as members of the United States Congress, Davis and Benjamin had once argued so fiercely that they seemed likely to duel, Benjamin soon became Davis's trusted advisor.

Once these appointments were made, the Cabinet members began to hire their own staff members, working to build the new nation's bureaucracy. In the meantime, the Provisional Congress continued to work on writing the first laws of the Confederate States of America. Its founders had also intended the new Confederate government to include a judicial branch, along with its executive and legislative arms. However, a Supreme Court was never established in the Confederacy, because members of the Confederate Congress could never reach an agreement about how much authority the Supreme Court should hold over individual state courts.[20]

The Capital

By March 1, 1861, the capital of the Confederate States of America—Montgomery, Alabama—hummed with activity. The Montgomery convention had held its meetings in a hotel, and it continued to do so after it became the Provisional Congress, until the Alabama House of Representatives lent it quarters. The small city did not have enough offices to house the new

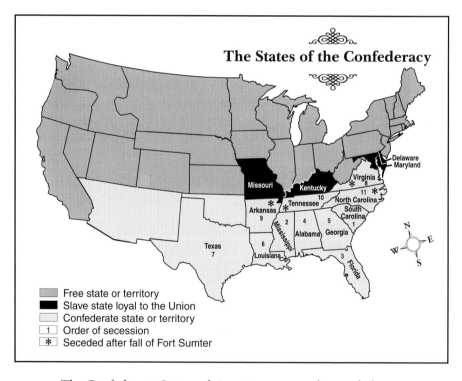

The Confederate States of America was made up of eleven states. While the Confederate government also recognized Kentucky and Missouri, the two border states were never under complete Confederate control.

government bureaucracy. A simple piece of paper on the door marked the president's office. The secretary of the treasury had to buy his own desk.

For a time, no Confederate flag flew in Montgomery. The Bonnie Blue flag flew over the Montgomery convention. The rectangular flag featured a white star in a field of dark blue. The Provisional Congress did not immediately choose a flag for the Confederacy. A committee was established and considered suggestions from the public about how the Confederate flag should look.[21] On March 4, 1861, the official flag flew for the first time. Known as the Stars and Bars, it featured three horizontal stripes, two red separated by one white. In its upper left corner, a circle of stars appeared on a field of blue. At first, this circle contained seven stars. After the last state seceded from the Union, it included thirteen stars (two of these represented Kentucky and Missouri, states that officially remained in the Union through the war). This flag was replaced, however, after it was mistaken on the battlefield for the United States flag.

The Confederate government would continue to adopt new flags throughout the war. In many ways, the failure of the Confederacy to wave just one flag seemed to symbolize the state of the government in general. Historian Wilfred Yearns described it as a "Trial and Error Government" in its earliest days, which was not surprising for a government that had to hurry to get up and running in the face of a huge, impending crisis.[22]

4

THE WORKINGS OF THE CONFEDERATE GOVERNMENT

Barely two months into its existence, everything changed for the new Confederate government. By firing on Fort Sumter, the Confederacy declared war on the United States, a much stronger, better-armed nation. On April 12, 1861, the Confederate government increased its preparations for war. What had been a flurry of activity became a frenzy.

Expanded Confederacy

Government duties expanded greatly in the spring of 1861 as more states joined the Confederacy. Virginia entered the Confederacy in April. North Carolina, Tennessee, and Arkansas joined in May. This brought the number of states in the Confederacy to eleven.

Four border slave states—Maryland, Delaware, Kentucky, and Missouri—stayed in the Union, as did the new state of West Virginia, formed in 1863 from counties that had formerly been part of Virginia. In

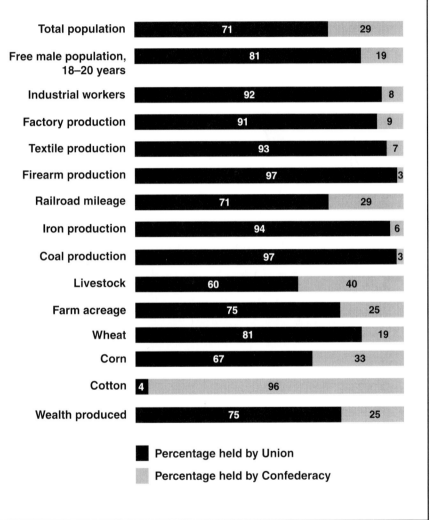

Resources of the
Union and Confederacy, 1861

Total population	71 / 29
Free male population, 18–20 years	81 / 19
Industrial workers	92 / 8
Factory production	91 / 9
Textile production	93 / 7
Firearm production	97 / 3
Railroad mileage	71 / 29
Iron production	94 / 6
Coal production	97 / 3
Livestock	60 / 40
Farm acreage	75 / 25
Wheat	81 / 19
Corn	67 / 33
Cotton	4 / 96
Wealth produced	75 / 25

■ Percentage held by Union

▨ Percentage held by Confederacy

When the Civil War began, the new Confederate nation was up against a much stronger opponent. This graph compares the resources of the Union and the Confederacy.

some cases, the Union used force to keep border states in the Union.

In Missouri, following the firing on Fort Sumter, an "intrastate civil war" broke out.[1] Both Union and Confederate regiments formed there. Troops faithful to the Union cause attacked a pro-Southern militia near St. Louis. The governor of Missouri, Claibourne Jackson, became a Confederate. In October, he called for a meeting of the legislature in Neosho, rather than the capital of Jefferson City. The group that answered his call became a rump assembly.[2] It voted for secession. On November 29, the Confederate Congress passed a resolution admitting Missouri. However, the government it recognized remained in exile throughout the war. Unionists continued to run another state government, so the United States also claimed the state.

Kentucky, on the other hand, declared itself neutral. After Confederate troops invaded Kentucky in September 1861, the official state government declared its loyalty to the Union. Another rump government formed, however. It voted to secede and won recognition from the Confederacy.[3] Representatives from both Kentucky and Missouri sat in the Confederate Congress, despite the fact that the official state governments remained part of the Union.

Richmond, the New Capital

Even before the state of Virginia formally joined the Confederacy, Confederate officials had begun to discuss the possibility of moving the new nation's capital to Richmond, Virginia, a large city close to the United States capital at Washington, D.C. Montgomery, Alabama, was proving too small to accommodate the new government. Its location would also prove inconvenient during the war—it was simply too far from the front where the fighting took place. Messages from the government would take too long to reach army officials. The South's only ironworks capable of producing heavy arms was located in Richmond, which would be convenient for the secretary of war, who would need to oversee production. Finally, members of the government wanted to reward Virginia for joining the Confederacy. When the officials decided to locate the capital there, they acknowledged what a rich and powerful state Virginia was.[4]

On April 27, Virginia's secession convention formally invited the Confederate government to move its capital to Richmond. On May 11, the Provisional Congress voted for the change.[5] Ten days later, it adjourned its second session. Then, about one thousand government employees—members of Congress, Cabinet members, and many clerks—packed their bags. President Jefferson Davis left Montgomery on May 29. As his train made its way toward Richmond, crowds gathered at every station to cheer him. The nation's spirits ran high.[6]

After the government arrived in Richmond, almost all its energy was devoted to war preparations. The Confederate Army was organized. The secretary of war appointed generals and other army officials.

Fortunately for the South, many of its citizens had years of experience in the United States Army. Just as many Southern congressmen had left seats in the United States Congress to take new seats in the Confederate Congress, Southern officers in the United States Army had quickly switched allegiance to the South. Robert E. Lee, who would eventually become the supreme commander of the Confederate Army, offered to lend his sword to the cause—to fight for the Confederacy—as did many other great soldiers.

Regiment after regiment of volunteers marched to Richmond. From there, they would be sent to camps mainly between Richmond and the Virginia-Maryland border.[7] President Davis and his top advisors met and devised the Confederacy's war strategy. For the most part, the plan was simply to defend the nation from invading Union troops. The Confederacy would let the Union cross its borders and then fight. If the occasion arose, Confederate forces would also look for opportunities to strike—but their main goal would be to destroy invading forces and hope that Northerners would eventually tire of having their men killed on Southern soil and decide to quit fighting.[8] The Confederacy, in other words, was not fighting to conquer the North, but to be left alone.

Manassas (Bull Run)

For close to three months after the battle at Fort Sumter, the Confederate Army conducted what historian Emory M. Thomas called "the dress rehearsal for war."[9]

Its soldiers organized and drilled. In the meantime, the Union Army concentrated its efforts on laying plans to capture Richmond. Seize the capital, the Union reasoned, and the Confederacy would collapse. In the summer, United States forces began to put these plans into effect.

Early in July, Union General Irvin McDowell led an army out of Washington, D.C., toward the Confederates' main position near Manassas Junction, behind a stream named Bull Run. The Confederacy called the battle that took place there the First Battle of Manassas, following its general policy of naming battles after towns. The Union, which named battles after landmarks, called it the First Battle of Bull Run. By the end of this first real battle, the Southerners had forced the Northerners to withdraw. The victory gave the Confederacy great hope that the South would succeed in keeping the North from forcing the seceded states back into the Union.

General Election

By the fall of 1861, Richmond remained safe, and the Confederates' hopes for victory stayed high. It was time to establish a permanent government. A general election was held in November 1861. When Jefferson Davis had become the new nation's provisional president nine months earlier, he was elected to the office by only forty-three men, the delegates at the Montgomery convention. In this new, general election, the public reelected him for a full six-year term.[10]

Members of the first Confederate Congress were also chosen in this election. The Congress was made up of 28 senators and 122 representatives. Every member of the Confederate Congress was a white male, just as in the United States Congress at that time. Most were rich planters or professionals. Almost one third of those elected to the first Confederate Congress had served in the United States Congress before secession. Others had been members of state legislatures.

Like the members of the Cabinet, Confederate congressmen faced daunting tasks. The crises that faced their country were numerous and complicated. The country's lack of political parties proved unfortunate, because it meant that politicians were not guided by party platforms. As the war went on, politicians did break into opposing groups, mainly over the issue of how they felt about Jefferson Davis. At the start, however, the Confederacy had no formal political parties. They owed no loyalty to any particular group. As historian Steven A. Channing wrote, "each legislator voted his whim on every issue."[11] Every bill that was introduced met opposition.

Dissent

Dissent frequently broke out in the political arena. As time passed, many members of the public began to feel angry toward the government of the Confederate States of America. Fighting a war against an established country such as the United States was a difficult and expensive task for a brand-new nation such as the

Confederacy. The war created great hardship in the people's everyday lives. The government seemed powerless to aid the public, to curb inflation, or to provide basic necessities. The public did not like some of the sacrifices they were called upon to make. They also resented actions the government took that directly affected them—the passage of income tax and draft laws, in particular.[12]

Many people—both members of the public and politicians—specifically criticized President Jefferson Davis. Even Vice President Stephens spoke out against him. Davis's Cabinet also came under fire. In Congress, representatives became so angry with one another on a few occasions that fistfights broke out.[13] To avoid hostile public criticism, congressional sessions were secret. At least one newspaper, the Richmond *Examiner*, speculated that this was because congressmen spent their time drinking whiskey.[14] In the spring of 1862, when reports circulated that the Union Army might soon invade Richmond, Congress adjourned to avoid capture by Union troops. Many Southerners labeled its members cowards, though a new session opened on August 18, 1862.

Over the years of the war, disagreement became extremely intense in parts of the Confederacy. Some historians have gone so far as to claim that there were "internal" civil wars being fought in addition to the one between the North and the South. In fact, in places all over the Confederate states, there were

TO THE

Citizens of the State,

AND THE

PEOPLE of RICHMOND

THE ENEMY UNDOUBTEDLY

ARE APPROACHING THE CITY !

And may be expected at any hour, with a view to its capture, its pillage, and its destruction. The strongest considerations of self and of duty to the country,

CALL EVERY MAN TO ARMS !

A duty which none can refuse without dishonor. All persons, therefore, able to wield a musket, will immediately

Assemble upon the Public Square

Where a regiment will be found in arms, and around which all can rally, and where the requisite directions will be given for arming and equipping those who respond to this call.

☞ **The Governor confidently relies that this appeal will not be made in vain.**

WM. SMITH,

GOVERNOR OF VIRGINIA.

Fearing invasion by Northern troops, Southern papers printed headlines like this one, calling for additional troops to join the Confederate ranks and to protect Southern property.

groups of people who actively supported the Union and hoped to see the defeat of the Confederacy.

Achievements

Despite the criticism, however, the Confederate government did have some real achievements. In the face of adversity, politicians and bureaucrats managed to build and support the Confederate Army. They also managed the Confederacy's ports, roads, and railroads, encouraged its industry, and represented it in negotiations with foreign nations. And it did all this while fighting a fierce war against a much wealthier, stronger opponent.

The Treasury

Confederate money was controlled by the secretary of the treasury and Congress. The war required a tremendous amount of money and remained a problem throughout the Confederacy's life. To put money in the treasury at the beginning of the war, the Confederacy had seized Union assets. It also issued bonds and took out loans.

When these measures did not generate enough revenue, the treasury started printing paper money. During the war, states, counties, railroads, and merchants also printed money.[15] Crooks added counterfeit money to the large amount already in circulation. Printing money on such a huge scale led to inflation. At the beginning of the war, a Confederate dollar was worth 95 cents in gold. By 1863, the dollar's value had fallen to 33 cents.

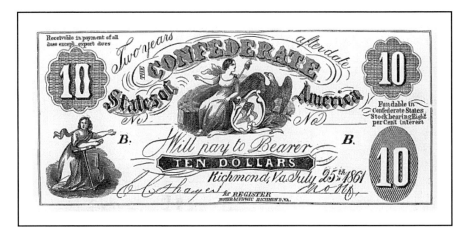

The Confederate government issued bonds and paper money to try to raise revenue to fight the war.

On May 1, 1865, its value had fallen to less than a tenth of one cent. Twelve hundred Confederate paper dollars could be traded for one dollar in gold.[16]

Armament

The government also handled the manufacturing of war supplies. The secretary of war and his Ordnance Bureau, the government agency in charge of providing war supplies, including weapons and ammunition, oversaw the Richmond Armory and Arsenal. Throughout the war, the arsenal provided about half of the ordnance material the army was issued. Its productions included more than 1,500 cannons, 350,000 muskets and carbines, and 72 million rounds of small arms ammunition.[17] The government Powder Works at Augusta, Georgia, also contributed greatly to the war effort. It produced more than 7,000 pounds of gunpowder per day throughout the war.[18] There was also a government arsenal in Atlanta that manufactured arms. The army's Quartermaster Department acquired cloth and produced huge numbers of uniforms, blankets, hats, and shoes. The Commissary Department collected and distributed the military's food.

Transportation

One major challenge the Confederate government faced was the Union naval blockade of Southern ports. Abraham Lincoln initially ordered twenty-six steamers to patrol the four thousand miles of Confederate coast, obviously an impossible task.[19] Eventually, the Union spent millions of dollars on what historian Burke Davis called "the first modern effort to strangle a nation by naval blockade."[20] The blockade that had started out shakily gradually became strong. Some historians believe it was the blockade that "brought the South to its knees."[21]

The blockade greatly affected the Confederacy's foreign trade, particularly toward the end of the war. It made it hard for the South to sell its major crop—cotton—overseas, which prevented the Confederacy from making the money it needed so badly to function. In 1861, the Union Navy stopped one out of ten blockade runners—Confederate ships that tried to smuggle goods past the blockade—headed for the Southern coast. By 1865, the Union was able to stop one out of two blockade runners.[22]

Besides the problems with sea transportation, the Confederacy had difficulty with land travel. When the war broke out, there were far fewer railroads in the South than in the North. Nevertheless, the military depended on what Southern railroads there were to move troops and supplies. If railroad travel were hindered by a lack of money or by military battles, the Confederacy would be crippled in its effort to continue the war. Railroad companies controlled Confederate railroads for most of the Civil War. By the end of the war, however, the government also assumed their control.

The Post Office

The Post Office Department, which was established as part of the Confederate government, proved to be one of the most successful of all its agencies. The Confederate Constitution required the post office to become self-supporting within two years of its establishment. In fact, it was the only federal agency in either the Confederate States or the United States to profit during the war years.

To make it profitable, Postmaster General John H. Reagan took what today would seem extreme measures. At first, he had Confederate post offices simply sell Union stamps, saving enormous printing costs. Later, the Confederacy did print its own stamps. For a time, Confederate postmasters made their own stamps. Reagan eventually arranged for the owners of a New York bank note company to sneak out of the United

States and into the Confederacy, where they started engraving for the Confederate cause. When the Post Office Department started to print stamps bearing a picture of Jefferson Davis, it made postal history. Never before or since in American history has a stamp honored someone still alive.[23] Twice, Reagan doubled postal rates. He took away congressmen's franking privileges, which had allowed them to send mail for free. He also made contracts with railroads that let the mail be shipped at low rates, and he persuaded army officials to grant post office employees immunity from the draft.[24]

Propaganda

During the war, the Confederate government sometimes deliberately spread propaganda. Some was designed to mislead Union government officials and army officers about war plans. Other propaganda, however, was used to bolster public morale.

The Confederate Congress passed censorship laws and issued army orders that prohibited newspapers from informing their readers where troops were concentrated or moving.[25] Newspaper editors, however, broke the rules and sometimes printed military campaign plans and blockade runners' schedules. On the other hand, newspaper editors also tried to boost morale by running commentaries on the relative strengths of the Union and the Confederacy. Journalists often described Union soldiers as cowards, despite evidence to the contrary. Sometimes newspapers also published reports that were simply wrong, claiming victories in battles that were actually defeats in an effort to prevent Southerners from finding out how desperate a situation they actually faced.

Foreign Relations

As in the United States, in the Confederacy, the secretary of state was in charge of foreign relations. When the Civil War broke out, the Confederacy hoped to form alliances with England and France. Southerners believed their cause was righteous and thought this would be seen as an obvious truth in Europe, which had recently experienced many revolutions of its own.[26] Confederates also believed that England, in particular, would support the South rather than the North because it relied so heavily on Southern cotton. When the Civil War broke out, England had a huge milling industry. Twelve hundred English factories and mills produced a vast amount of cotton fabric, which was sold all over the world.[27]

The Confederacy soon discovered, however, that forming alliances was much more difficult than it had anticipated. England would not agree to intervene directly in the war—to provide soldiers or ships to the Confederacy, for example. However, individual Englishmen did trade huge amounts of military goods for cotton. France also remained officially neutral. For a time, it looked as though England and France would reach an agreement to enter the war together on the side of the South. But after Abraham Lincoln issued his Emancipation Proclamation, which freed the slaves in the Confederate states (but not in the Union), in January 1863, emancipation became a Union war goal. This led both the British and French, who opposed slavery, to decide that, morally, they could not fight for the Confederacy.[28]

Throughout the war, the Confederacy sent diplomats to Europe, hoping to make an alliance or gain diplomatic recognition. Other individuals also went to Europe to plead the Confederate cause. In 1863, when loyal secessionist and Confederate spy Rose O'Neal Greenhow traveled to Europe, she discovered that most members of the ruling classes sympathized with the Confederates.[29] Greenhow even met French Emperor Napoleon III, but nothing came of it.

The Confederacy also worked hard to build diplomatic relations with Mexico. John T. Pickett was the Confederate commissioner who went to Mexico City. He found, however, that the government was pro-Union. Mexican officials remembered all too well the many occasions when Southerners had tried to grab Mexican land—for example, in the Mexican War of 1846.

Ultimately, the Confederacy would stand alone in its fight.

5

LIFE IN TOWN AND COUNTRY

The eleven states of the Confederate States of America had a total population of 9 million, including 3.5 million slaves.[1] In 1860, only a relatively small number—just 24 percent—of the South's white population were members of slave-owning families.[2] Moreover, half of all slave owners owned fewer than five slaves. The new nation's population included only about twenty-three hundred families that owned more than a hundred slaves. This "planter aristocracy" formed a tremendously vocal political group and contributed an enormous amount to the South's economy, but constituted less than one percent of the Confederacy's total population.[3] About half of the total population belonged to middle-class farming families. Two million were poor whites who eked out a meager living from the land.[4]

The Civil War profoundly changed the Confederacy's population. Some Southerners left farming and became industrialists, in response to the demands of war.[5] Women formed a new working class as they

The Civil War drastically changed the lives of those in the Southern planter aristocracy, such as Virginia landowner John Minor Botts (seated, at center), seen on the porch with his family in 1861.

stepped into jobs vacated by men who had joined the army.

But the greatest changes were brought about by the emancipation of the slaves and on the battlefield. Ultimately, 80 percent of the Confederacy's white men of military age—800,000 men—enlisted as soldiers in the Confederate Army. By contrast, only 50 percent of the Union's eligible white men of military age served. By the end of the war, 258,000 Confederate soldiers had died, more than half of them from disease rather than on the battlefield. In general, more Confederate wounded soldiers died than Union wounded because the Confederate medical service was inferior to that of the Union.[6]

By the end of the war, the Confederate Army included draftees, as well as volunteers. Most Confederate soldiers were single, Protestant white men from the country, natives of the South. The Confederate Army included boys and old men. Eventually, draft laws required men up to age fifty to serve in the army. The draft was especially notable (and resented by Confederates) because, in the South, the government had always interfered as little as possible in the lives of its citizens.[7]

The Confederate Experience

Southerner Lucy Buck wrote in 1862, "We shall never any of us be the same as we have been."[8] Seemingly all Confederates suffered hardships at some point during the Civil War, but degrees of suffering often varied according to people's social status and where they lived. Clearly, the poor—including slaves—sacrificed the most. Residents of areas invaded by the Union Army faced the greatest physical danger. Often they lost virtually all their worldly possessions when they became refugees, fleeing their homes as the Union Army was approaching. As a whole, Southerners suffered more than Northerners in the Civil War, mainly because almost all Civil War battles were fought on Southern soil.

A Patriotic Fervor

At first, white Southerners generally greeted news of the outbreak of war and the formation of the Confederacy with joy. One slave, watching rebel troops march off to war, commented, "They sing and whoop, they laugh: they holler to de people on de ground and sing out 'Good-bye.' All going down to die."[9] Soldiers and civilians alike were sure the war would provide chances for adventure and glory. Southerners expected the Confederate Army to enjoy decisive victories in a few battles and then watch the Union surrender after a short war. Divisiveness soon appeared, however. Attitudes changed as the Confederacy began to lose battles and people realized that this would be no short, easy war.

The Southern Economy

Before the war, the South had a stable, agrarian economy. Cotton production helped the region to prosper. When the war broke out, the Confederacy had little industry. To make war supplies for the army, the new country had to develop a new industrial base quickly. Southerners immediately began to manufacture many products. Within a year after the start of the war, factories were producing cloth, uniforms, tents, rope, leather, saddles, candles, cots, plows, stoves, paper, steam engines, guns, cannons, swords, and spurs.[10] Joseph Reid Anderson, the owner of a huge ironworks located in Richmond, Virginia, expanded his business after the war began and started to run coal mines, a tannery, a sawmill, and a brick factory as well. He also purchased a blockade runner and nine canal boats to transport the goods his companies manufactured.[11] Cities all over the South experienced manufacturing booms.

Nevertheless, the war shattered the South's economy. Altogether, the South would lose 60 percent of its assets during the war.[12] By the end of the war, farms and plantations were able to sell very little in the way of crops. Their production had dramatically fallen off, partly because so many men had left to fight and were not around to oversee the plantations. The people— often women—who ran the farms and plantations during the war lacked supplies and transportation. What they did manage to grow was often seized by invading Union forces or taken by the Confederate government for the use of the army. Some of what farmers produced rotted because it could not be shipped.

Life in the Cities

After the formation of the Confederacy, industry developed rapidly in cities to produce supplies and ammunition for the war. But hard times quickly followed in all but the largest cities—those with the most government contracts. Many small industries foundered. Their owners ran out of money or could not acquire raw materials because of the blockade or other transportation problems. Some sold out to larger companies.[13]

Throughout the war, skilled laborers—carpenters, machinists, blacksmiths—could always find work.

White-collar workers were also needed as managers, foremen, and clerks in government offices. But people who had to flee their homes when the Union Army approached had particular trouble finding jobs. They arrived in strange cities, looking for work and a safe place to stay.

Southern city dwellers began to suffer from scarcity and inflation. Money fell into short supply—partly because, in order to acquire funds, the government issued war bonds, which the public bought. War bonds soaked up most of the public's gold and silver. Especially after the Confederacy printed a great deal of paper money, inflation soared. During the war, prices in the Union increased by about 80 percent. Prices in the Confederacy, on the other hand, increased by a whopping 9,000 percent. In 1864, citizens paid forty-six dollars for the same items that had cost just one dollar in 1861.[14]

To cope with rising prices, in the summer of 1864, Jefferson Davis ordered all enlisted men's salaries increased by $7 per month, which meant that privates in the infantry and artillery would earn $18 per month. This seemingly huge increase did families very little good. Prices had risen so much that $18 would pay for just one peck of cornmeal or two pounds of bacon. A pair of shoes cost close to $100.[15] In 1865, butter cost $25 a pound and wood $100 a load. Toward the end of the war, a woman living in Richmond reported: "Close times in this beleaguered city. You can carry your money in your market basket and bring home your provisions in your purse."[16]

An employee in the War Department, John Beauchamp Jones, made $3,000 a year. His son, Curtis, made the same. Despite their combined income of $6,000, Jones wrote on July 17, 1863, "We are in a half-starving condition. I have lost twenty pounds and my wife and children are emaciated to some extent."[17] In 1864, the family earned $10,200, yet Jones could afford just one ounce of meat a day for each family member. On January 24, 1865, he wrote in his diary, "What I fear is starvation."[18] Within two years, Jones died—in part due to malnutrition.

Secretary of the Treasury Christopher Memminger tried to finance the war by selling bonds and raising taxes. But the public could not afford enough bonds and resisted tax legislation strongly, so he had to order more and more money printed. By the end of 1863, the country had $730 million in circulation. By the end of the war, the Confederacy had issued more than $1.5 billion in paper money. Such printing caused paper money to depreciate in value especially quickly.

Blockade runners did manage to bring some goods to the South. Between November 1863 and December 1864, for example, they delivered more than 8 million pounds of meat and 500,000 pounds of coffee to the Confederacy.[19] Nevertheless, basic necessities like ink, paper, needles, pins, nails, screws, plates, cups, and kettles ran out. City dwellers learned to make do, to improvise and invent what they needed—boot polish and hairpins, for instance. A lack of doctors and medicines also led people to rely on homemade medicines.

Eventually, a barter economy developed. As people ran out of money, they started to trade among themselves for things they needed. People also bartered because they did not want Confederate paper money— they preferred to collect debts in goods. Sometimes people simply learned to do without what they might have considered necessities before the war.

For residents of Richmond, Virginia, life became especially exciting during the war years. Residents did experience shortages, but for a long time, the city did not experience such severe shortages as elsewhere. Rich women continued to throw glamorous parties, where they served fine food and liquor that blockade runners had brought from the Caribbean and Europe. At the end of the war, however, things would take a definite turn for the worse. The Union Army kept Richmond under siege for nine months before invading and burning much of the city.

Life in the Country

On the surface, Confederates who lived in the country generally owned less property than did those in the city. But they proved lucky. They were poorer, but they suffered less, largely because farmers could grow their own food. Women living on farms had experience spinning, weaving, and sewing, which they had often done before the war. Therefore, families in the country could more easily manufacture the things they needed at home.

Nevertheless, life was hard in the country, too. As young men marched off to war, women, children, and old men had to take over the farming. The army was in constant need of horses, so few were left to be used as work animals. It became difficult to have tools or machines repaired—blacksmiths and replacement parts were constantly in short supply.

After 1861, many farmers stopped planting tobacco and cotton and instead started to grow food in their fields.[20] Even so, Confederate soldiers often went hungry, despite the fact that farmers grew ample food. Food grown on Confederate farms often failed to be delivered to troops in the field because of inadequate transportation, mismanagement, speculation, hoarding, and a lack of salt (to prevent meat from spoiling).[21] All over the Confederacy, people suffered from a lack of things they had once considered necessities: coffee, flour, sugar, salt, paper, and lamp oil.

After 1863, farmers suffered when the Impressment Act authorized army officers to seize part of what farmers grew.[22] Collectors took one tenth of all the wheat, corn, cotton, sugar, tobacco, and other crops.[23] Farmers, as well as plantation owners, also suffered at the hands of Union invaders. By the end of the war, Union soldiers had slaughtered 40 percent of the South's livestock and destroyed half of its farm machinery.[24]

Life on the Plantations

Toward the beginning of the war, plantation families usually suffered less than others. They had stockpiles of supplies and equipment. They had money. Slaves continued to work in their fields and their houses.

Some plantation owners lived in comfort throughout the war. In areas the Union Army reached, however, planters suffered terribly. Soldiers ransacked their houses, barns, and fields. Sometimes they burned plantation homes. They confiscated horses and mules as work animals and killed pigs, cows, and chickens for food. With the arrival of the army, slaves often fled behind Union lines, seeking the precious freedom they had been denied so long. Some Union Army officers encouraged their men to do extra damage to prominent planters' property. In fact, invasion caused demoralization and destruction everywhere.

Getting the News

Newspaper readership rose especially high during the war, as people sought news of battles and the loss of loved ones. Journalists, however, found it hard to find out what was going on inside the Confederate government, because Congress took steps to keep many of its actions secret. The most important function newspapers served was printing casualty lists—the names of those soldiers who had died or been wounded in battle.

Confederates also kept track of what was going on through correspondence. Mail was exchanged between soldiers and civilians. Even illiterate soldiers sent news home by having others write for them. The problem, however, was in delivery. Sometimes it took months for letters to be delivered. Telegraph lines also carried messages between government officials and army staff and between soldiers and their families.

Popular Diversions

Letters and diaries from the time reveal that, despite the hardship, Confederates continued to indulge in a variety of popular diversions throughout the war. Many plays were performed for large audiences in towns and cities. When there were not enough actors available to fill male roles, women stepped in, using costumes and makeup to take men's parts. Minstrels made the rounds of towns. Confederates also liked to watch organ-grinders, jugglers, and tumblers. In both cities and small towns, women raised money for good causes by presenting charades.

People also went to dinner parties, picnics, sing-alongs, and candy pulls. Men continued to fish and hunt. Men and women played cards, although a shortage of cards meant that players sometimes had to make their own decks.

Observance of holidays also continued. Many Southerners gave up celebrating the Fourth of July, but families continued to celebrate Christmas. Mothers made toys for their children.

Flight

By the end of the war, invading Union soldiers were in control of two thirds of Confederate land, totaling approximately 500,000 square miles.[25] Tens of thousands of Confederates took flight, abandoning their homes. Usually these refugees headed for cities. The arrival of large numbers of refugees in Southern cities made shortages especially severe there.

Confederate soldiers, of course, suffered most in terms of death and disease. In other ways, however, Confederates who did not fight suffered as much as those who went to the battlefield.

6

WOMEN OF THE CONFEDERACY

Many Confederate women displayed mixed feelings at the onset of the Civil War. They felt a mixture of sadness, fear, and pride as they watched soldiers march off. Many felt their cause was just. Schoolgirl Sarah Strickler wrote in her diary: "Virginia used every honourable means to preserve this once glorious union; but when she found her efforts in vain sadly withdrew from the tottering fabric & joined her destinies."[1] At the beginning, most seemed to believe that the Confederacy would triumph. Certainly no one could have foreseen the tragic losses their new country would suffer.

Women generally accepted their new duties. They stepped into new roles. The greatest torment they suffered was in not knowing exactly where the soldiers they loved were. Even when they knew, they sometimes had to wait for weeks or months for news from a battlefield, to find out if their husband or son had died or was wounded or captured.

Confederate women made great sacrifices during the war. By the end, many no longer felt as patriotic as

Women played an important role in the Civil War in a variety of ways, from making clothes for soldiers to actually taking part in battle.

they had in the beginning. By then, they no longer saw the war as romantic. They felt exhaustion and despair. Historian Drew Gilpin Faust argued that, eventually, Confederate women came to exhibit self-interest. Mary Scales, for example, upon learning that her youngest son was to be drafted into the Confederate Army, wrote to the secretary of war to protest, saying,

> I know my country needs all her children and I had thought I could submit to her requisitions. I have given her cause my prayers, my time, my means [money] and my children but now the last lamb of the fold [her son] is to be taken, the mother and helpless woman triumph over the patriot.[2]

Combatants

At the onset of war, however, almost all Southern women supported the cause of the Confederacy with great enthusiasm. After the firing on Fort Sumter, some women formed their own military companies and practiced shooting, preparing to defend themselves in case of invasion. Adana Bocock of Fincastle, Virginia, wrote in a letter that students at a local

Confederate women tried to help soldiers by smuggling much needed medicines such as quinine past the Union blockade beneath their skirts.

women's academy had formed a military unit called the Female Dare Devils.[3]

A few Confederate women even disguised themselves as men and fought on battlefields. Barbara Ann Durvan of Tennessee died in a prison in Alton, Illinois, one of the Confederate soldiers captured by the Union Army.[4] How many other Confederate soldiers were actually women will never be known. Civil War re-enactor Lauren Cook Burgess became especially interested in female soldiers' stories after the National Park Service banned her from reenactments, claiming she lacked "authenticity." By 1994, she had found accounts of 135 women who fought in the Civil War for either the Union or the Confederacy.[5] Historian Mary E. Massey estimated that about four hundred women disguised themselves as soldiers and fought in the Civil War.[6] Almost all managed to escape detection. In the relatively few cases in which their secret was revealed, the discovery took place when they were injured or became ill and had to be examined by a doctor.

How did so many disguise their true identity? Neither the Confederate nor the Union Army required recruits to undergo a thorough physical examination. Also, most of the women who fought came from rural areas and already knew how to ride a horse and handle a rifle. Poor women and those who lived on farms were usually accustomed to physical labor. In camp, they ran little risk of discovery. In the nineteenth century, modesty was a way of life, so men as well as women would have resisted sharing latrines. It also would not have occurred to most men that anyone wearing pants could possibly be a woman. The norms of the day dictated that women should wear long dresses and elaborate hairstyles. In addition, many male soldiers were so young that they lacked facial hair, and their voices had yet to change.

Some newspaper stories about women soldiers did appear during the Civil War. Journalists often wrote kind words about women who followed brothers or husbands into the army or expressed extremely patriotic views. Other women, however, were branded immoral.[7]

Spies, Scouts, and Smugglers

Confederate women served as spies as well as soldiers. Rose O'Neal Greenhow acted as a spy in Washington, D.C. She was a prominent hostess in the capital before and during the war. Union officers confided many secrets to her. She was imprisoned by the Union after she sent Confederate General P.G.T. Beauregard information about Union plans to advance on Manassas in July 1861. Because of the information she provided, Confederate President Jefferson Davis credited her with the South's victory there.[8] After serving two prison terms, Greenhow was exiled to the Confederacy. She then traveled to Europe to raise money for the Confederate cause. She died in 1864 on her return voyage. The Confederacy awarded her full military honors when she was buried.

Rose O'Neal Greenhow, seen here with her daughter, was a wealthy and fashionable Washington, D.C., hostess. She was able to use her friendships with Union military and political figures to obtain information that she later passed along to the Confederates.

Perhaps the most famous female Confederate spy, however, was Belle Boyd. She became a spy at the age of seventeen, after Union soldiers invaded her hometown of Martinsburg, Virginia (now in West Virginia). At parties, she listened to Union soldiers and passed on what she learned of their plans to Confederate officials. Eventually, she ran a spy ring.

In May 1862, Boyd was living in Port Royal, Virginia, when Union forces began to lay plans to burn nearby bridges, thereby preventing easy Confederate access to Washington, D.C. After Boyd learned of these plans by eavesdropping on Union General James Shield, she told Confederate General Stonewall Jackson, who took advantage of the information and hurried his approach to Washington.[9] Union forces returning to Port Royal arrested Boyd, who was sent to the federal prison in Washington. She was eventually released as part of a prisoner exchange.

During the war, she was arrested on six occasions and put in prison twice. After her last release from prison, she sailed on a blockade runner for Europe, carrying secret dispatches from the Confederate government. Her ship was seized by a Union Navy ship, but en route to New York, she captured the Union captain, Samuel Hardinge, and fled to London. Boyd and Hardinge later married. When Hardinge returned to the United States, he was arrested on charges of treason. He was eventually released, but soon died. After the war, Belle Boyd wrote her memoirs and became a stage actress.[10]

Belle Boyd, a young Confederate spy, passed important information to General Stonewall Jackson. In later years, she became an actress, making a living by recounting her wartime experiences.

Another teenager, Emma Sansom, once acted as a scout for Confederate General Nathan B. Forrest in Georgia. Forrest had planned to use a particular bridge to cross Black Creek, but found it burning. Sansom clambered up onto Forrest's horse behind him and directed him to a ford, a low place where he could easily cross the creek without the bridge.

Women also engaged in smuggling for the Confederate cause. Louisa P. Buckner was stopped by Union guards as she crossed the border from Washington, D.C., into the Confederate state of Virginia. When they discovered she was carrying quinine, a medicine, inside her skirts, she was thrown into prison. When General Gabriel J. Rains of the Confederate Torpedo Bureau needed wire for bombs he was manufacturing, it was women who sneaked behind enemy lines to steal it.[11]

Other Important War Work

One crucial role Confederate women played in the Civil War was as nurses. Today we think of nursing as largely a female profession, but women had begun to enter the field only in the 1850s. Some nurses worked in improvised hospitals near battlefields. Sometimes they actually ventured onto battlefields to rescue or treat wounded soldiers. Alabama nurse Juliet Opie Hopkins, a wealthy widow who had sold a huge amount of real estate in order to raise funds for Confederate hospitals, came into the line of fire and was shot twice on the battlefield.[12] She played such an important part in the war effort that her picture appeared on currency printed in her home state. Other women staffed hospitals far from the front, where the wounded were sent to recover. After battles, women flocked to aid however they could. Constance Cary, who became a nurse when a battle was fought near her home, remembered her experience. As she watched, "During the night began the ghostly procession of wounded brought in from the field."[13]

Nursing the wounded was hardly a simple matter of bathing foreheads and administering medicine. Nurses had to help doctors amputate limbs and treat huge, gaping wounds. Years later, Phoebe Yates Pember remembered holding her finger on a young boy's artery to stop his hemorrhaging. When she fainted and fell to the floor, he died.[14] Jefferson Davis so admired one nurse, Sally Tompkins, that he made her a captain in the Confederate Army. She ran a hospital she had started herself.

As the war progressed, women also began to take over jobs that had earlier been filled by men. They went to work in offices like those of the Confederate Treasury, the Quartermaster's Department, the Ordnance Department, and the Post Office. They also worked in factories, helping manufacture ammunition. Some found employment in textile mills.

Women also manufactured items such as socks and shirts, both as individuals and as members of societies. In fact, women organized many aid societies in the Confederacy. The Lynchburg Hospital Association not

Sally Tompkins was one of the best known nurses for the Confederate Army. Her tireless efforts won her the recognition of Confederate President Jefferson Davis.

only raised money for medical supplies but also ran a food drive.[15]

Women sewed the flags carried by military units. When fabric became scarce, they sometimes made flags out of their own dresses. When a unit prepared to march, women threw parties and organized religious services. They gathered along the street to cheer the troops as they went off to war. Confederate Private Milton Barrett wrote, "We left camp . . . we was cherd [cheered] all the way by crowd of sitercens [citizens], a flag was waven [waving] over most every house and every winder [window] was crowded with ladys [*sic*]."[16] When troops arrived in a town, the local women considered it their duty to entertain them. A girl named Cordelia Scales wrote to a friend that about fifty soldiers came to visit her family every day—to talk, sing, and play parlor games.[17]

Life at Home

The war forced most Confederate women to work harder and longer than ever before. In rural areas, women planted and tended the crops. Some women had to take over the running of plantations. They supervised slaves in the fields and sometimes labored themselves. Anne Gorman Justice kept her family's small plantation going while her husband was away in the army. In her letters, she wrote about planting and harvesting crops, measuring corn, soaking wheat, slaughtering pigs, cutting wood, spinning, weaving, and sewing.[18] Other women tanned leather and dug under their old smokehouses for dirt from which they could extract salt. They pickled vegetables. They packed up boxes of food to send soldiers. They tried to answer requests from soldiers for clothing, especially shoes, shirts, and socks.

During the Civil War, fashion underwent drastic changes due to a scarcity of materials and imports. Most women had to make their own clothes. They learned to make their own hats from palmetto and straw and decorate them with bits and pieces of ribbon and lace. Lucky women had animals with hides they could tan for leather to make shoes. Those without leather made shoes out of canvas. Some even used glue and paper to make shoes. Many women ended the war barefoot.[19]

Historian Bell Irvin Wiley contended that, in some ways, the war actually brought upper-class women freedom. They became less bound by custom and tradition. Some found useful work for the first time in their lives.[20]

Other women, however, suffered to such an extent that some wrote to their husbands, begging them to come home. Many soldiers deserted the Confederate Army and went home when their families' situation became desperate.[21] In Salisbury, North Carolina, in March 1863, women crazed by their need for food for their families formed an angry mob and stormed the local railroad depot, demanding the flour that was stored there. The next month, women also rioted in Richmond, Virginia. A mob of about a thousand

BUTLER'S PROCLAMATION.

His outrageous insult to the Women of New Orleans!

Southern Men, avenge their wrongs !!!

Head-Quarters, Department of the Gulf, New Orleans, May 15, 1862.

General Orders, No. 28.

As the Officers and Soldiers of the United States have been subject to repeated insults from the women calling themselves ladies of New Orleans, in return for the most scrupulous non-interference and courtesy on our part, it is ordered that hereafter when any Female shall, by word, gesture, or movement, insult or show contempt for any officer or soldier of the United States, she shall be regarded and held liable to be treated as a woman of the town plying her avocation.

By command of Maj.-Gen. BUTLER,

GEORGE C. STRONG,

A. A. G. Chief of Stables.

Confederate women faced not only hardship and loss of loved ones. In some instances, they also felt their dignity insulted. For example, in Union-occupied areas of Louisiana, General Benjamin Butler issued this proclamation. It stated that women who cheered or showed their support for the Confederacy by criticizing the Union in public would be arrested as prostitutes.

women and boys looted stores near Capitol Square. They stopped only when Jefferson Davis himself appeared, vowing to share his last crust of bread with any who suffered.[22]

Motherhood and Marriage

War proved especially difficult for mothers, who sometimes found themselves the sole support of large families. Their children missed the fathers and brothers who had gone away to fight. Those born after their fathers went to war might reach the age of four before ever meeting them. And of course, many children lost their fathers in the war. Mothers had to do what they could to console children in their grief, even while dealing with their own and continuing to provide.

Many marriages took place during the Civil War. Both men and women sought comfort in romance. Many wanted to cement their relationships before soldiers left to fight.

Invasion and Flight

In areas where the Union Army invaded, Confederate women especially suffered. Union soldiers sometimes entered their homes and seized their property. Some women, however, did form friendships with Union soldiers.

Following the Union invasion, many Confederate women chose to flee from their homes. They simply packed what belongings they could and fled. Some fugitives from Tennessee, Arkansas, Louisiana, and

Mississippi went all the way to Texas. People who lived on the coast in Alabama, Georgia, and the Carolinas or along the Union-Confederate border in Virginia moved to the interiors of those states.[23] These refugees often had a great deal of trouble finding new homes. In many places, the only homes available for rent were extremely expensive, so the poor and the middle class had to make do, some even living in sheds.

7

AFRICAN AMERICANS IN THE CONFEDERACY

When the Civil War broke out, 3.5 million African-American slaves lived in the states of the Confederacy, along with about 261,918 free blacks.[1] For two hundred years, African Americans in the South had suffered greatly. Slave families were often very strong. Members loved and tried to protect one another. But these families were also extremely fragile because slave owners often broke them up, selling them off separately. Even "humanitarian" owners interfered in slaves' childrearing. Owners named slave children, decided what kind of education—if any— slaves would receive, and to a certain extent, determined what religion slaves would follow. Some owners and overseers raped slaves. Slaves were also subjected to whippings and forced to work extremely hard.

When word began to spread of the war, most slaves hoped, naturally, that the Union would win and that they would gain their freedom. Booker T. Washington, who was born a slave and would grow up to become a famous educator, remembered waking up at night during his childhood and overhearing his mother "fervently praying that Lincoln and his armies might be successful and that one day she and her children might be free."[2]

The Union Army

Two hundred fifty thousand blacks lived north of the Mason-Dixon line when the Civil War broke out. They have been credited as acting as "a whip and a spur," working hard to increase commitment to the abolitionist cause among members of the Lincoln administration.[3]

In all, 180,000 black soldiers fought for the Union Army in the Civil War.[4] At first, army officials refused to use them. By 1863, however, Union military officials' attitudes toward black soldiers had changed. Governor John A. Andrew of Massachusetts started a movement to enlist blacks in the Union Army. Recruiters, among them famous abolitionist and former slave Frederick Douglass, eventually signed up one thousand black men from every state in the Union for the Massachusetts 54th Regiment.[5] On the day these troops marched through Boston, twenty thousand people lined the streets to watch them.

However, most of the blacks who served in the Union Army during the Civil War were actually Southerners. Within two weeks of the attack on Fort Sumter, escaped slaves began to cross Union lines.[6] Among the earliest to join the Union cause were three slaves belonging to Stephen Mallory. He had sent these men to Sewall's Point, on the coast of Virginia, to help build a battery. There, they seem to have stolen a boat and rowed across Chesapeake Bay to Union Fortress Monroe. A picket guard opened the gate to let them in. The next morning, they were taken to meet General Benjamin F. Butler, who immediately put them to work building a bakery. Soon, a messenger arrived under a flag of truce, sent by Mallory. He requested that the slaves be returned to him. Butler told him, "I shall detain the Negroes as contraband of war."[7] *Contraband* refers to goods or property a nation at war seizes from its enemy. In the Civil War, the Union used the term to refer to former slaves Union forces had taken from Southerners, or who had run away to the protection of Union troops. In labeling slaves contraband, the North used the Confederates' definition of slaves as property against them.

The news that Butler had refused to return runaway slaves quickly spread among local slaves. Within three days, more than sixty slaves arrived at Fortress Monroe. The number only grew. Up and down the Southern coast, slaves stole boats and rowed out to vessels in the Union Navy's blockade. A few slaves had themselves shipped north in freight containers, by wagon or train.

Other slaves also joined the Union Army. Some simply followed the army as it marched through the South. Northern officials recorded that when they arrived in Accomac and Northampton counties in Virginia they experienced "an almost stampede of slaves."[8] When the Union Army arrived on the coast of

Southern slaves who crossed the Union lines into freedom were called contrabands. The Union used the South's argument that slaves were property against the Confederacy by taking slaves away from their owners, calling them contraband, or illegal, property.

Georgia, fifteen thousand slaves joined it.[9] Perhaps the most spectacular escape was that of Robert Smalls, a slave who had been working on a boat in Charleston Bay. On May 12, 1862, he led a party of sixteen slaves onto the *Planter* and stole it. He piloted the boat away and turned it over to the Union Navy.[10]

As joyful as they were to be free, many slaves who joined the Union Army experienced great hardship. They suffered greatly from hunger and disease. Many died for the Union cause. As many as five hundred thousand ex-slaves sought protection from the Union Army after fleeing their owners.

The Confederate Army

When the war broke out, many of the free blacks living in the South offered to do war work for their states. For example, a group of free blacks left Petersburg, Virginia, in April 1861 to work on fortifications in Norfolk. Three hundred volunteered to help fortify the harbor at Hampton.[11] Individuals also donated money and supplies to the Confederate cause. Jordan Chase of Vicksburg gave a horse to the cavalry and five hundred dollars to the government.[12] Many other free blacks tried to enlist in the Confederate Army. State and local officials let blacks help build fortifications, but their offers to bear arms were rejected everywhere except New Orleans. Even in Louisiana, the two black regiments formed never actually fought.[13]

Historian Benjamin Quarles offered several reasons free blacks threw their support behind the Southern war effort, including a sense of patriotism:

> Like thousands of white Southerners who personally hated slavery and felt that it was doomed with the coming of the war but who nevertheless defended the Confederacy, these free Negroes had a sense of community responsibility which impelled them to throw their lot with their neighbors.[14]

Others went to work, Quarles explained, because defense jobs paid well. Some hoped that, if free blacks participated in the war, the Confederate government would be less inclined to pass hostile legislation restricting their rights. Quarles has suggested one reason that Confederate officials never permitted free blacks to bear arms in defense of their country: "To in any way officially raise the status of the free Negro would have repercussions in the form of additional slave discontent."[15]

Male slaves were used in great numbers in the war effort. Six Confederate states passed legislation under which governors could impress slaves for military service, meaning that the government could force owners to send their slaves to work on war-related projects. This legislation did not provide for use of slaves in combat. Slaves impressed by states usually built fortifications and battlements. The states paid their owners for their labor. The Confederate Army also impressed slaves. General J. Bankhead Magruder of the Army of the Peninsula issued orders on September 7, 1861, for owners to deliver to him half of their slaves.[16] They were supposed to arrive equipped with tools such as spades and shovels. Some slaves also worked as attendants in Confederate Army field hospitals. One general remarked that these slave laborers accomplished twice what the same number of white workers would do. After all, slaves were used to hard physical labor and long days.

Many slaves went to war with their masters as personal body servants. They found food and cooked for their masters, took care of their equipment, and cleaned their quarters. Some slaves risked their lives. During battles, they went out on the field to find their wounded masters and carry them to safety. On September 19, 1864, Confederate Lieutenant George

Whitaker Wills of the 43rd Carolina Regiment died at Fisher's Hill. His slave, Wash, wrote a letter of condolence to his master's brother, Richard Wills. Wash tried to comfort the Wills family, saying:

> I am glad to tell you that his coat was buttoned up in the prettiest style of uniform and in his breast pocket was his little Testament. . . . We talked over everything, troubles sorrow and sicknesses. . . . He said he never went in any battle with the expectation of coming out safe, he seemed then to give himself up into the hands of Providence. . . . Master Richard, I believe it as much as I ever believed anything in my life, that he is at rest, my heart believes it. . . .[17]

Toward the end of his letter, Wash indicated that he was then planning to start serving another member of the family and said, "I am willing to do anything I can do to help out our struggling country. . . ."[18] Unlike Wash, however, some slaves who accompanied their masters to battle fled behind Union lines as soon as possible.

Toward the end of the war, when the Confederate Army found few new recruits, a great debate broke out among Confederate leaders about whether slaves should be allowed to join the Confederate Army as soldiers. In November 1864, President Jefferson Davis asked Congress to authorize the purchase of forty thousand slaves whom he proposed to free after they had served in a military workforce. He went so far as to say that, once there were no longer enough white men to serve in the army, these black men could become soldiers.[19]

In February 1865, Confederate Secretary of State Judah P. Benjamin came under fire from many members of the public when he spoke out in favor of not only enlisting slaves in the army, but offering freedom to any slave who volunteered for military service. He argued that the North's use of black soldiers had forced the South "to [choose] whether the negroes shall fight for or against us."[20] On the other hand, Howell Cobb of Georgia expressed the sentiments of many others when he wrote to the Confederate secretary of war on January 8, 1865: "The day you make soldiers of them is the beginning of the end of the revolution. If slaves will make good soldiers, our whole theory of slavery is wrong."[21]

Soon Confederate General Robert E. Lee publicly came out in favor of recruiting and freeing slaves. Congress then passed bills authorizing their enlistment. President Jefferson Davis signed the law on March 13, 1865. Within weeks, black companies were parading on Capitol Square in Richmond. The government considered their members now free men. Presumably this was the reason so many slaves had volunteered their service. Ironically, the war ended so soon afterward that none of these soldiers actually made it to the battlefield.

Slaves at Home

At the start of war, most slaves continued to work incredibly hard every day. Some masters permitted their slaves to work in cities in war industries or on the railroads. Slaves who lived on farms and plantations still worked in the fields, although now they generally planted and tended food crops rather than cash crops such as cotton or tobacco. To supply soldiers and deal with shortages, they also began to tan leather, make soap, and boil seawater to make salt. Like their owners, slaves suffered from shortages of food during the Civil War. They also found themselves ill-clothed by the end of the war.

As their masters left for war, some slaves ran away. Thousands are believed to have migrated north even before Union troops arrived in their neighborhoods.[22] Other slaves simply refused to work, believing Union forces would free them and punish their masters. Some slaves who had served a family for a long time on a plantation remained loyal throughout the war, taking great care to protect women and children. Despite the tenderness with which many slaves treated the families that owned them, however, it should not necessarily be assumed that they did not also want freedom.[23]

Throughout the war, many slave owners tried to control their slaves through lies designed to generate fear. Masters told slaves that the Union would sell runaway slaves they found to Cuba. The Norfolk *Day Book* newspaper went so far as to print an article saying that Union soldiers harnessed black men like oxen and forced them to haul stone.[24] Slave owners also controlled slaves by moving them from towns to the country when Union troops approached, to keep them as far as possible from the Union soldiers who might liberate them or encourage them to run away.

Despite their owners' attempts to keep them ill-informed, throughout the war, slaves often had methods they used to keep apprised of war news. They eavesdropped on owners' conversations, read newspapers (if they could read), and passed on what they learned to other slaves.

Uprisings

Southern whites had always feared the possibility of a violent revolt by the black slaves, who sometimes outnumbered the whites. This fear was as present as ever during the Civil War. To prevent this, the Confederacy passed new laws designed to prevent blacks from obtaining firearms and liquor during the war. Slave owners voluntarily mounted patrols during the war, riding out at night to make sure slaves were not out and about. Slaves in town had to carry passes. Laws also prevented blacks from assembling unless white people were present.

To prevent free blacks from inciting slaves to escape, laws prevented them from owning or hiring slaves. During the war, several states also passed laws prohibiting the freeing of slaves. Although many of these precautions had been taken for years before the Civil War, the Union threat made a slave revolt seem even more dangerous. So efforts to control slaves were strengthened as much as wartime allowed.

Slaves and the Union Invasion

Whenever Union troops approached, slaves living on farms and plantations began to run away. Union soldiers wrote home over and over again about the cheering and shouting that went up when they first appeared.[25] In May 1863, troops commanded by Union General Ulysses S. Grant captured Port Gibson, Mississippi. One planter from the area wrote that, as soon as Union forces approached, "the fetters of slavery were broken instantly, and the hoe and plow handle dropped from the hands of the negroes, and I ceased to be a planter forever. It is amazing with what intuitive familiarity the negroes recognized the moment of deliverance. . . ."[26] Within days, forty-three slaves had escaped from his plantation. Only thirteen, of whom

Slaves often joined the invading Union troops as they passed Southern plantations.

eight were children, remained. Some slaves who remained with their masters after the Union invasion did so only because their masters agreed to start paying them for their labor.

Slaves greatly helped Union troops by supplying them with information about Confederate troop movements and local geography—the location of roads and bridges, for example. Some slaves led Union soldiers to their masters' hidden valuables. Others helped Union soldiers who had escaped capture find their way back to the relative safety of Union lines.

Emancipation Proclamation

On January 1, 1863, President Abraham Lincoln's Emancipation Proclamation went into effect. It declared all slaves in areas rebelling against the United States "forever free." Lincoln made the proclamation in his capacity as Commander in Chief of the Union military forces. It was not a moral pronouncement, based on Lincoln's feelings against slavery. Instead, it was a war measure, designed to encourage Confederate states to come back to the Union.

The proclamation, first introduced in September 1862, did not free the slaves in states that had remained in the Union, or the areas in the Confederacy that Union forces had invaded and now controlled. In effect, then, Lincoln's proclamation did not free any slaves in the areas over which the Union had control. And its authority in the states of the Confederacy was, at best, limited. Its purpose, however, was to encourage

SOURCE DOCUMENT

Despite his popularity among blacks and abolitionists for issuing the Emancipation Proclamation, Abraham Lincoln did have his enemies in the North. This 1864 political cartoon shows Democratic presidential candidate and former Union General George McClellan saving the Union from Abraham Lincoln and Confederate President Jefferson Davis.

the Confederacy to give up the war—to reenter the Union *with* their slaves (at least temporarily).

In reality, however, the proclamation changed the goal of the war. No longer was it simply a fight to restore the Union as it was. Now it was a fight to free the slaves. Slaves throughout the South, as well as free blacks and abolitionists in the North, greeted news of the Emancipation Proclamation with great joy, believing it was the first real step on the road to the abolition of slavery.

By early March 1865, General Robert E. Lee realized that his Confederate army was bound to lose. On a visit home, he told his son Custis that soon Confederates "will repent."[1] His troops knew it, too. The Confederate Army was suffering greatly from desertions. Hundreds of soldiers waited each day for nightfall and then slipped away, heading home. Those who remained with the army suffered more and more, as supplies ran short. Many trains had stopped running, making resupply nearly impossible. Nevertheless, Lee continued to fight.

THE LEGACY OF THE CONFEDERACY

The Fall of the Confederacy

History often records April 9, 1865, as the date the Confederacy ceased to exist. On that day, General Robert E. Lee surrendered what remained of his army to Union General Ulysses S. Grant at Appomattox Court House, Virginia. A week earlier, General Grant had begun a campaign to get behind the Confederate Army of Northern Virginia in that state. The arrival of Union forces had caused the evacuation of the cities of

Richmond and Petersburg. Even the government of the Confederacy had abandoned the capital. Lee had tried to unite his force of approximately thirty thousand men with that of General Joseph E. Johnston by heading south, but Union troops forced them west instead. At Sayler's Creek, thousands of Confederate soldiers were captured.

Finally, at the crossroads village of Appomattox Court House, Union forces surrounded Lee's troops. With forces in front of them, behind them, and on either flank, Lee had no way to flee, and his troops were too weak to fight. Half of Lee's men no longer had weapons. They had run out of food. If he wanted to continue to fight, Lee's only option was to order his men to disband, to flee for the hills, and continue the war as guerrillas (small units of soldiers who harass the enemy by staging surprise raids). Some Confederates would have supported him in this decision, but Lee decided it would cost his countrymen too much.

Just as the Union infantry and cavalry lined up for a final assault on the Confederate Army, a horseman galloped from behind the Confederate lines. He was bearing a staff topped with a white flag of surrender. Suddenly, all fell quiet. The fighting in Virginia had come to an end.

Lee and Grant met at a nearby house. Grant told Lee the terms of surrender. The Confederate soldiers were simply to stop fighting and go home. They would not be stopped by Union authorities. Those who owned their horses could take them. Officers

Even though he knew by early March 1865 that defeat was inevitable, Confederate General Robert E. Lee continued to fight for another month until forced to surrender.

could take their side arms and personal possessions, too. In offering these generous terms, Grant granted Lee what historian Bruce Catton called a "good peace."[2] Grant promised Lee that the United States would not seek to punish or execute for treason those who had fought for the Confederacy. Lee himself would not be hanged, nor would any of his subordinates. Grant offered Lee twenty-five thousand rations to feed his troops. Then, a member of Grant's staff wrote out the articles of surrender, and the two generals signed them.[3] Three days later, Confederate General John B. Gordon and his twenty thousand men also surrendered.

Davis Flees

For a month and a day after Lee's surrender, Jefferson Davis tried to keep the Confederacy alive. He and five members of his Cabinet fled Richmond on April 2, before Lee's surrender. Earlier, he had helped his wife pack and sent her south, along with their children, her sister, three slaves, and daughters of a friend. When they parted, he told her he thought it was very likely he would not live to see her again. "I don't expect to survive the destruction of constitutional liberty," she remembered his telling her.[4]

Davis and his Cabinet began their flight from the capital after receiving a telegram from Lee, saying that he expected soon to have to abandon his position. Lee wrote, "I advise that all preparations be made for leaving Richmond to-night. . . ."[5] After he read the

After it became evident that the Confederate Army would be defeated, Jefferson Davis sent his wife, Varina, and their children (seen here) south. Davis did not expect to live to see his family again.

telegram, Davis first went to church and then called a meeting of the Cabinet at noon. He ordered them to pack up essential government papers. All others would be burned. They agreed to meet at the train station at 7:00 P.M.

When he went home to pack, Davis discovered that some of his slaves had taken the opportunity to flee. He gathered together a few necessities, leaving behind many of his family's prized possessions. He sent a messenger to the bank to cash a check he had received from a recent auction of many of the Davises' household goods and silver. The bank, however, refused to cash the check, and Davis was forced to flee with only a five-dollar gold piece, a fat roll of almost worthless Confederate paper money, and the uncashed check.

Davis and his Cabinet headed south on the presidential train that night. Although the men carried very few personal belongings with them, the train was well stocked. Once the party reached safety, the refugee government could begin work once more. That night, Richmond burned as retreating Confederates set fire to the armory to prevent Union forces from using its supplies. Shells exploded and conditions in the city were simply too chaotic for the fire to be put out. The following morning, the first Union soldiers rode into the city.

In the meantime, Davis's train took him and the Cabinet south. On April 3, they got off at Danville, Virginia, where they stayed through April 10, after hearing the news of Lee's surrender and that Union troops were approaching. They had to abandon Danville, too, and fast.

Once again, they packed their few belongings and met at the railroad station to leave for Greensboro, North Carolina. Greensboro townspeople greeted the arrival of Davis and the others without enthusiasm. Later, the Cabinet members remembered that no one wanted to provide them rooms. People feared being punished for helping the fleeing Confederates when Union troops arrived. Davis found a bed, but the other government officials spent most of their days in the railroad car.

In Greensboro, Davis met with Confederate Generals P.G.T. Beauregard and Joseph E. Johnston. He tried to persuade them to raise a new army and continue to fight. Davis believed the Confederacy could still survive and continue the war by rallying the troops beyond the Mississippi River. Just after this meeting, Davis received a message from Lee outlining the terms of his surrender. This seems to have been when Davis learned that, while Confederate soldiers would be pardoned for their role in the war, he and the members of his Cabinet were excluded from this arrangement.[6]

Davis could not decide what to do next. He listened to a plan proposed by John Taylor Wood, who wanted him to head for Florida, where he could board a ship for Texas. Confederate General Edmund Kirby Smith was even then raising a force of fifteen thousand troops for Davis to lead into Mexico, where he could regroup Confederate soldiers and continue to fight.[7]

On April 14, Davis bought horses and wagons. The following day, his party started out. They would ride cross-country through the Carolinas and into Georgia. On the road, Davis learned of the assassination of President Lincoln by a fanatical Confederate sympathizer named John Wilkes Booth. Davis's family joined him en route.

On April 24, in Charlotte, North Carolina, the Cabinet held its last formal meeting. By now, Union soldiers were pursuing them. Obviously false rumors were circulating through the United States that Davis was carrying a vast fortune with him. The Davis party continued to hope to make it over the Mississippi River. They failed.

On May 10, 1865, Union soldiers captured Davis outside Irwinville, Georgia.[8] It was the death blow to the Confederate States of America.[9] Union soldiers took Davis as a prisoner to Savannah, Georgia, where he was put on board a ship bound for Washington, D.C. Over the next two years, while Davis remained imprisoned, Americans debated whether he should be put to death as a traitor. Eventually, he was released. He would spend the rest of his life mourning the loss of the Confederacy and trying to regain the honor and reputation he had lost during the war.

To this day, historians debate Jefferson Davis's effectiveness as Confederate president and to what extent he was responsible for the fall of the Confederacy. A tall, gaunt, nervous man, plagued throughout his life with ill health, Davis was extremely formal by nature. He found it hard to relax except with family and thus, often had trouble communicating with other government officials. Some have labeled him a failure, blaming his cold personality and his stubborn refusal to admit when he was wrong for the trouble he had persuading other officials to carry out his instructions. Others, however, have argued that he faced a challenge no man could have met. Historian Bell Irvin Wiley pointed out as Davis's particular strengths his distinguished political and military experience, his appeal to the public (he was an excellent public speaker), his incredible sense of duty, and his complete devotion to the Southern cause.[10]

Release of Prisoners of War

Following Lee's surrender, soldiers were released from prison camps in both the North and the South. Early in the war, the United States and the Confederacy had regularly exchanged prisoners of war. In later years, however, Union General Grant had discontinued prisoner exchanges. Grant realized that the exchanges just reinforced the Confederate Army, which was running short of men.

Conditions in both Northern and Southern prison camps were awful. In the words of historian Bruce Catton, "They were overcrowded, reeking from lack of sanitation, badly policed; housing was bad, food was worse, and medical care was sometimes worst of all."[11] Close to fifty thousand men died in these camps, most from disease or malnutrition. Some simply succumbed to despair. Union prisoners at the Confederate camp called Andersonville, in Georgia, suffered perhaps the most extreme conditions. Photographs show men housed there so starved that they literally resembled skeletons with flesh. Andersonville was so terrible, in fact, that its commander, Henry Wirz, was later tried in court for his cruel treatment of prisoners.

Soldiers Return Home

Those soldiers who were not prisoners of war also began to return home. Most traveled on foot, without supplies. They arrived home hungry and filthy. Many had suffered hideous wounds during the war. When gangrene threatened to kill soldiers, their limbs had been amputated.

Confederate soldiers sometimes had trouble locating their families, especially those who had fled from the invading Union troops. White refugees remained on the move. There were also many black refugees—former slaves—on the road, looking for work and a new place to settle. Some former slaves returned to the farms and plantations where they had lived and worked, looking for friends and family. Soldiers sometimes arrived home to find their families suffering terribly. Many were desperately poor. Houses and fields had been burned. The railroads were in ruins, having been destroyed by the Union Army.

A few thousand former planters were so devastated by the loss of the Old South, the Confederacy, and their old way of life that they left the country rather than face living under the Union they had fought. Many relocated to Europe and Mexico. Quite a few went to Brazil, where small communities of former planters started new lives as slaveholders once again.

The Aftermath: Reconstruction

From the end of the war in 1865 until 1877, the South underwent Reconstruction—a slow process by which

Confederate women mourn the loss of their loved ones in a New Orleans cemetery. Almost every Southern family experienced some loss during the course of the Civil War.

the former Confederate states were allowed to return to the Union, after meeting certain requirements set by the North. Before his death, President Abraham Lincoln had developed his own plans for Reconstruction. His initial plan called for a Southern state to be allowed to enter the Union with a new state government when a relatively small number of citizens—10 percent of the number who had voted in the presidential election of 1860—took an oath of allegiance to the United States. Lincoln also created categories of people he thought should have to receive a special presidential pardon before they would be allowed to take the oath of allegiance, including military officers and Confederate government officials—those who had led the South in its rebellion. Lincoln's fellow Republicans thought his plan was too weak, however. They proposed instead what was passed by Congress as the Wade-Davis bill in July 1864. This plan called for 50 percent (instead of 10 percent) of eligible voters to take the oath of allegiance before a Southern state would be allowed to reenter the Union. Lincoln never signed the Wade-Davis bill into law. At the end of the war, a new plan for Reconstruction had yet to be adopted. There had, however, been one very significant development. In a speech in April 1865, Lincoln revealed that he believed that some black men, at least, should be given the right to vote.

After Lincoln's assassination, the vice president, Andrew Johnson became president. Almost immediately he announced his own plan for Reconstruction. By this time, Reconstruction governments had been established in Texas, Virginia, Arkansas, and Louisiana, all of which were occupied by Union Army troops. Under Johnson's liberal program, presidential pardons were granted to many rich planters. By the end of 1865, all the former Confederate states had new civil governments.

In December of that year, the Thirteenth Amendment, which abolished slavery, was ratified and became part of the Constitution. In April 1866, Congress adopted the Fourteenth Amendment, which declared that all people born or naturalized in the

United States were its citizens. This meant all black Americans were citizens. The Fourteenth Amendment also pressed states to give black men the vote by stating that if a state did not do so, its representation in Congress would be reduced. It required a two-thirds vote on the part of Congress before men who had held political office before the war and sided with the Confederacy could hold state or national office.

The Fourteenth Amendment signaled Congress's growing dissatisfaction with Johnson's Reconstruction. When a new Congress convened in March 1867, it included a very large number of Republicans. Radical Republicans supported black suffrage and extended military occupation of the South, among other things. The Reconstruction Act Congress passed after a presidential veto in March 1867 invalidated all the new Southern state governments formed except for that of Tennessee (which had ratified the Fourteenth Amendment, unlike other Southern states, and had been readmitted to the Union).

The Reconstruction Act of 1867 granted black men the vote. What was called Congressional Reconstruction began in the spring of 1867. New Southern state governments were formed after state constitutional conventions were held. Republicans gained political control in the South. Blacks held many political offices, for the first time in the history of the United States. In 1868, six former Confederate states were readmitted to the United States. In 1870, the last four—Texas, Georgia, Mississippi, and Virginia—rejoined the Union.

THE THIRTEENTH AMENDMENT

SECTION 1. NEITHER SLAVERY NOR INVOLUNTARY SERVITUDE, EXCEPT AS PUNISHMENT FOR CRIME WHEREOF THE PARTY SHALL HAVE BEEN DULY CONVICTED, SHALL EXIST WITHIN THE UNITED STATES, OR ANY PLACE SUBJECT TO THEIR JURISDICTION.

THE FOURTEENTH AMENDMENT

SECTION 1. ALL PERSONS BORN OR NATURALIZED IN THE UNITED STATES, AND SUBJECT TO THE JURISDICTION THEREOF, ARE CITIZENS OF THE UNITED STATES AND OF THE STATE WHEREIN THEY RESIDE. NO STATE SHALL MAKE OR ENFORCE ANY LAW WHICH SHALL ABRIDGE THE PRIVILEGES OR IMMUNITIES OF CITIZENS OF THE UNITED STATES; NOR SHALL ANY STATE DEPRIVE ANY PERSON OF LIFE, LIBERTY, OR PROPERTY, WITHOUT DUE PROCESS OF THE LAW; NOR DENY TO ANY PERSON WITHIN ITS JURISDICTION THE EQUAL PROTECTION OF THE LAWS.

THE FIFTEENTH AMENDMENT

SECTION 1. THE RIGHT OF CITIZENS OF THE UNITED STATES TO VOTE SHALL NOT BE DENIED OR ABRIDGED BY THE UNITED STATES OR BY ANY STATE ON ACCOUNT OF RACE, COLOR, OR PREVIOUS CONDITION OF SERVITUDE.[12]

The Thirteenth, Fourteenth, and Fifteenth amendments to the United States Constitution, passed during Reconstruction, were designed to give the former slaves civil rights. They are collectively known as the Civil War amendments.

A Republican plan then reorganized their governments. Reconstruction did not end until 1877.

Remembering the Civil War

Many Americans remain fascinated by the Confederacy and the Civil War. But Civil War buffs do far more than read about their favorite era in American history. Dressed in replicas of the Union Army's blue and the Confederate Army's gray uniforms, people also reenact many of the war's greatest battles.

In towns and cities across the South, monuments to the Confederacy still stand today. The federal government maintains many Civil War sites as national parks. In 1948, the federal government paid to construct a copy of the Wilmer McLean House in Appomattox, Virginia, where Generals Ulysses S. Grant and Robert E. Lee negotiated the terms of the Confederate surrender.[13] Every year, thousands of tourists also visit the Museum of the Confederacy in Richmond, Virginia. Artifacts from the Confederacy are on display in many other museums as well, including the Smithsonian Institution in Washington, D.C.

Despite the popularity of the Civil War, some controversy does exist concerning the legacy of the Confederacy. At its heart, the Confederacy was a government set up to guarantee white people the right to own black people—a notion that seems unbelievable today. After the war, former Confederates worked hard to create a mythical idea of the "Old South," where people of all races lived happily side by side, despite the fact that one race held members of the other as slaves. This "Old South," however, never really existed, except in the minds of those who had fought for what they called the "Lost Cause." In World War II, some regiments carried the Confederate Stars and Bars. Another regiment carried the flag in the Korean War. In the 1960s, sales of the Confederate flag for a time almost equaled those of the Stars and Stripes (due to the centennial of the Civil War).[14] Segregationists often displayed the Confederate flag during the 1960s.

Today, many people consider collecting or displaying Confederate memorabilia inappropriate. Groups that display the Confederate flag have been severely criticized, because the display of the flag indicates, to many, support for slavery. In fact, racist groups have often adopted symbols of the Confederacy for their own use.

Despite the criticism, many Southerners, and even Northerners, continue to believe in an idealized vision of life in the South before the Civil War. They mourn the failure of what they call the "Lost Cause"—the Confederacy's independence from the United States.

★ TIMELINE ★

1619—Slaves brought to Jamestown, Virginia; Slavery begins in American colonies.

1793—Eli Whitney invents the cotton gin, which enables the South to become a cotton empire.

1820—Congress agrees on the Missouri Compromise, which allows Missouri to enter the Union as a slave state; The debate over whether slavery should exist in the United States is under way.

1854—The Kansas-Nebraska Act becomes law.

1857—The Supreme Court issues its decision in the *Dred Scott* case.

1859—John Brown tries to start a slave insurrection at Harpers Ferry.

1860—*November*: Abraham Lincoln is elected president of the United States.
December 20: South Carolina secedes from the United States.

1861—*February 1*: Delegates from six of the states that have seceded meet in Montgomery, Alabama.
February 4: The Montgomery convention votes to establish a new nation, the Confederate States of America.
February 8: Members of the Confederacy's Provisional Congress vote to adopt the Provisional Constitution of the Confederate States of America.
February 10: The Provisional Congress elects Jefferson Davis as president and Alexander Stephens as vice president of the Confederacy.
February 18: Davis is inaugurated.
April 12: Confederate forces bombard Union soldiers in Fort Sumter; The Civil War begins.

1863—*January 1*: United States President Abraham Lincoln issues the Emancipation Proclamation.

1865—*April 2*: Confederate President Jefferson Davis and his Cabinet evacuate the capital of Richmond.

April 9: General Robert E. Lee surrenders at Appomattox Court House, Virginia.

May 10: Davis is captured by Union soldiers; The Confederate States of America ceases to exist.

★ CHAPTER NOTES ★

Chapter 1. A New Nation at War

1. William C. Davis, *Brother Against Brother: The War Begins* (Alexandria, Va.: Time-Life Books, 1983), p. 147.

2. Emory M. Thomas, *The Confederate Nation, 1861–1865* (New York: Harper & Row, 1979), p. 67.

3. Benjamin Quarles, *The Negro in the Civil War*, 2nd ed. (Boston: Little, Brown and Company, 1969), p. 23.

4. Davis, pp. 136–137.

5. Geoffrey C. Ward, *The Civil War: An Illustrated History* (New York: Knopf, 1990), p. 36.

6. Quarles, p. 23.

7. Davis, p. 138.

8. Mary Chesnut, *A Diary From Dixie* (New York: Gramercy Books, 1997), p. 35.

9. Quarles, p. 23.

10. Ward, p. 39.

11. Quoted in Quarles, p. 24.

12. Ward, p. 42.

13. William C. Davis, *A Government of Our Own: The Making of the Confederacy* (New York: The Free Press, 1994), pp. 5, 224–225.

Chapter 2. Beginnings of the Confederacy

1. Bruce Catton, *The Penguin Book of the American Civil War* (Harmondsworth, England: Penguin Books, 1966), p. 7.

2. Peter Kolchin, *American Slavery, 1619–1877* (New York: Hill and Wang, 1993), p. 78.

3. Ibid., p. 79.

4. Catton, p. 9.

5. Kolchin, p. 194.

6. Paul S. Boyer et al., *Enduring Vision: A History of the American People* (Lexington, Mass.: D. C. Heath and Company, 1993), vol. 1, p. 316.

7. William C. Davis, *Brother Against Brother: The War Begins* (Alexandria, Va.: Time-Life Books, 1983), p. 38.

8. Boyer et al., p. 318.

9. Ibid., p. 320.

10. Catton, p. 12.

11. Henry Steele Commager, ed., "The Kansas-Nebraska Act," *Documents of American History*, 6th ed. (New York: Appleton-Century-Crofts, Inc., 1958), vol. 1, p. 332.

12. Davis, pp. 118–119.

Chapter 3. A New Nation Is Born

1. Emory M. Thomas, *The Confederate Nation, 1861–1865* (New York: Harper & Row, 1979), p. 42.

2. William R. Smith, *The History and Debates of the Convention of the People of Alabama . . . 1861* (Montgomery, Ala.: White, Pfister & Co., 1861), p. 131.

3. Thomas, p. 56.

4. Bell Irvin Wiley, *Embattled Confederates: An Illustrated History of Southerners at War* (New York: Harper & Row, 1964), p. 258.

5. Wilfred Buck Yearns, *The Confederate Congress* (Athens: The University of Georgia Press, 1960), p. 24.

6. William C. Davis, *Brother Against Brother: The War Begins* (Alexandria, Va.: Time-Life Books, 1983), p. 130.

7. Yearns, p. 29.

8. Ibid., p. 228.

9. Davis, p. 130.

10. Ibid., p. 128.

11. Ibid.

12. Quoted in Geoffrey C. Ward, *The Civil War: An Illustrated History* (New York: Alfred A. Knopf, 1990), p. 27.

13. Benjamin Quarles, *The Negro in the Civil War*, 2nd ed., (Boston: Little, Brown and Company, 1969), p. 43.

14. Thomas, p. 60.

15. Burke Davis, *The Civil War: Strange & Fascinating Facts* (New York: Fairfax Press, 1982), p. 184.

16. Wiley, p. 23.

17. Thomas, p. 81; Wiley, p. 25.

18. Wiley, p. 19.

19. Burke Davis, p. 187.

20. Steven A. Channing and the Editors of Time-Life, *Confederate Ordeal: The Southern Home Front* (Alexandria, Va.: Time-Life Books, 1984), p. 10.

21. Burke Davis, p. 193.

22. Yearns, p. 22.

Chapter 4. The Workings of the Confederate Government

1. Emory M. Thomas, *The Confederate Nation, 1861–1865* (New York: Harper & Row, 1979), p. 94.

2. Ibid.

3. Ibid.

4. Ibid., p. 100.

5. Ibid., pp. 99–100.

6. Ibid., p. 102.

7. Ibid., p. 110.

8. Ibid., p. 108.

9. Ibid., p. 103.

10. Bell Irvin Wiley, *Embattled Confederates: An Illustrated History of Southerners at War* (New York: Harper & Row, 1964), p. 13.

11. Steven A. Channing and the Editors of Time-Life, *The Confederate Ordeal: The Southern Home Front* (Alexandria, Va.: Time-Life Books, 1984), p. 11.

12. Ibid., p. 10.

13. Ibid., p. 13.

14. Ibid.

15. Burke Davis, *The Civil War: Strange & Fascinating Facts* (New York: Fairfax Press, 1982), p. 189.

16. Ibid., p. 190.

17. Wiley, p. 107.

18. Ibid., p. 109.

19. Davis, p. 40.

20. Ibid.

21. Ibid.

22. Ibid.

23. Ibid., p. 187.

24. Ibid.

25. Channing, p. 49.

26. Thomas, p. 169.

27. Thomas Boaz, *Guns for Cotton: England Arms the Confederacy* (Shippensburg, Pa.: Burd Street Press, 1996), p. 2.

28. Thomas, p. 181.

29. Duke University Special Collections Library, "Rose O'Neal Greenhow Papers at Duke," May 1996, <http://scriptorium.lib.duke.edu/greenhow> (March 10, 1999).

Chapter 5. Life in Town and Country

1. Paul S. Boyer et al., *Enduring Vision: A History of the American People* (Lexington, Mass.: D. C. Heath and Company, 1993), vol. 1, p. 484; Bell Irvin Wiley, *Embattled Confederates: An Illustrated History of Southerners at War* (New York: Harper & Row, 1964), p. 231.

2. John B. Boles, *Black Southerners, 1619–1869* (Lexington: University Press of Kentucky, 1983), p. 75.

3. Steven A. Channing and the Editors of Time-Life, *Confederate Ordeal: The Southern Home Front* (Alexandria, Va.: Time-Life Books, 1984), p. 8; Boles, p. 75.

4. Ibid., p. 8.

5. Emory M. Thomas, *The Confederate Nation, 1861–1865* (New York: Harper & Row, 1979), p. 212.

6. Quoted in Burke Davis, *The Civil War: Strange & Fascinating Facts* (New York: Fairfax Press, 1982), p. 215.

7. Boyer et al., p. 477.

8. The Museum of the Confederacy, "A People Apart," *The Museum of the Confederacy Newsletter*, Spring 1998, <http://www.moc.org> (March 10, 1999).

9. Quoted in Boyer et al., p. 477.

10. Wiley, p. 105.

11. Ibid., p. 107.

12. Boyer et al., p. 511.

13. Wiley, p. 112.

14. Boyer et al., p. 482.

15. Wiley, p. 87.

16. Quoted in Burke Davis, *The Long Surrender* (New York: Random House, 1985), p. 5.

17. Wiley, p. 114.

18. Ibid., p. 115.

19. Davis, *The Civil War: Strange & Fascinating Facts*, p. 42.

20. Wiley, p. 80.

21. Ibid.

22. Boyer et al., p. 479.

23. Wiley, p. 29.

24. Channing, p. 3.

25. Ibid.

Chapter 6. Women of the Confederacy

1. University of Virginia Library, *Hearts at Home: Southern Women in the Civil War*, September 1, 1997, <http://www.lib.virginia.edu/exhibits/hearts/patriot.html> (March 10, 1999).

2. Quoted in Drew Gilpin Faust, *Mothers of Invention: Women of the Slaveholding South in the American Civil War* (Chapel Hill: University of North Carolina Press, 1996), p. 241.

3. University of Virginia Library, *Hearts at Home: Southern Women in the Civil War.*

4. Ibid.

5. Lauren Cook Burgess, ed., *An Uncommon Soldier: The Civil War Letters of Sarah Rosetta Wakeman, Alias Private Lyons Wakeman, 153rd Regiment, New York Volunteers* (Pasadena, Md.: The Minerva Center, 1994), p. xii.

6. Mary Elizabeth Massey, *Women in the Civil War* (Lincoln: University of Nebraska Press, 1994), p. ix.

7. Burgess, p. 5.

8. Duke University Special Collections Library, "Rose O'Neal Greenhow Papers at Duke," May 1996, <http://scriptorium.lib.duke.edu/greenhow> (March 10, 1999).

9. Defense Equal Opportunity Management Institute, *Women in the Military*, July 1995, <http://www.pafb.af.mil/DEOMI/wommil95.htm> (March 10, 1999).

10. Faust, p. 218.

11. Burke Davis, *The Civil War: Strange & Fascinating Facts* (New York: Fairfax Press, 1982), p. 107.

12. University of Virginia Library, *Hearts at Home: Southern Women in the Civil War.*

13. The Museum of the Confederacy, *A People Apart—Museum of the Confederacy*, n.d., <http://www.moc.org/Articles/people.htm> (September 21, 1999).

14. Wiley, p. 95.

15. University of Virginia Library, *Hearts at Home: Southern Women in the Civil War.*

16. The Museum of the Confederacy, *Hope of 8 Million—Museum of the Confederacy*, n.d., <http://www.moc.org/Articles/Hopeof8mil.html> (September 21, 1999).

17. Wiley, p. 171.

18. Ibid., p. 170.

19. Ibid., pp. 81, 84, 176.

20. Ibid., p. 171.

21. Ibid., p. 182.

22. Davis, p. 117.

23. Wiley, pp. 178–179.

Chapter 7. African Americans in the Confederacy

1. John B. Boles, *Black Southerners, 1619–1869* (Lexington: University Press of Kentucky, 1983), p. 135.

2. Bell Irvin Wiley, *Embattled Confederates: An Illustrated History of Southerners at War* (New York: Harper & Row, 1964), p. 239.

3. Benjamin Quarles, *The Negro in the Civil War*, 2nd ed. (Boston: Little, Brown and Company, 1969), p. xi.

4. Ibid., p. 21.

5. Ibid., p. 9.

6. Ibid., p. 58.

7. Ibid., p. 60.

8. Ibid., p. 70.

9. Ibid., p. 71.

10. Ibid., p. 72.

11. Ibid., p. 36.

12. Ibid., p. 37.

13. Ibid., pp. 39, 40.

14. Ibid., p. 39.

15. Ibid., pp. 39, 40.

16. Ibid., p. 47.

17. Wiley, p. 235.

18. Ibid.

19. Emory M. Thomas, *The Confederate Nation, 1861–1865* (New York: Harper & Row, 1979), p. 291.

20. Wiley, p. 241.

21. Ibid.

22. Quarles, p. 56.

23. Ibid., p. 51.

24. Ibid., p. 46.

25. Ibid., pp. 54–55.

26. Wiley, p. 236.

Chapter 8. The Legacy of the Confederacy

1. Burke Davis, *The Long Surrender* (New York: Random House, 1985), p. 12.

2. Bruce Catton, *The Penguin Book of the American Civil War* (Harmondsworth, England: Penguin Books, 1966), p. 274.

3. Geoffrey C. Ward, *The Civil War: An Illustrated History* (New York: Knopf, 1990), p. 379.

4. Quoted in Davis, p. 14.

5. Davis, p. 19.

6. Ibid., p. 68.

7. Ibid., p. 69.

8. Ibid., p. 144.

9. Catton, p. 275.

10. Bell Irvin Wiley, *Embattled Confederates: An Illustrated History of Southerners at War* (New York: Harper & Row, 1964), pp. 13–14.

11. Catton, p. 228.

12. Geoffrey R. Stone et al., *Constitutional Law*, 2nd ed. (Boston: Little, Brown and Company, 1991), pp. lii–liii.

13. Burke Davis, *The Civil War: Strange & Fascinating Facts* (New York: Fairfax Press, 1982), p. 20.

14. Ibid., p. 223.

★ FURTHER READING ★

Books

Burch, Joann J. *Jefferson Davis: President of the Confederacy.* Springfield, N.J.: Enslow Publishers, Inc., 1998.

Channing, Steven A., and the Editors of Time-Life. *Confederate Ordeal: The Southern Home Front.* Alexandria, Va.: Time-Life Books, 1984.

Davis, Burke. *The Civil War: Strange & Fascinating Facts.* New York: Fairfax Press, 1982.

———. *The Long Surrender.* New York: Random House, 1985.

Davis, William C. *Brother Against Brother: The War Begins.* Alexandria, Va.: Time-Life Books, 1983.

———. *A Government of Our Own: The Making of the Confederacy.* New York: The Free Press, 1994.

Hull, Mary E. *The Union and the Civil War in American History.* Berkeley Heights, N.J.: Enslow Publishers, Inc., 2000.

Kent, Zachary. *The Civil War: "A House Divided."* Hillside, N.J.: Enslow Publishers, Inc., 1994.

Ward, Geoffrey C. *The Civil War: An Illustrated History.* New York: Alfred A. Knopf, 1990.

Internet Addresses

American Civil War Home Page. February 24, 1995. <http://sunsite.utk.edu/civil-war/warweb.html> (May 7, 1999).

Duke University. *Civil War Women Internet Resources.* n.d. <http://odyssey.lib.duke.edu/women/cwdocs.html> (August 28, 1999).

Williams, Kenneth H. *The Papers of Jefferson Davis.* April 9, 1996. <http://www.ruf.rice.edu/~pjdavis/> (August 27, 1999).

★ INDEX ★